A Call Towards Love

DANA LIBERTA
AND LORI WEAVER

ISBN 978-1-961017-75-7 (Paperback)
ISBN 978-1-961017-92-4 (Hardback)
ISBN 978-1-961017-76-4 (Ebook)

Inquiries and Book Orders should be addressed to:

Leavitt Peak Press
17901 Pioneer Blvd Ste L #298,
Artesia, California 90701
Phone #: 2092191548

A gift of *love is a*dmired for *e*ternity.

♥

A daughter is a mother's gender partner, her closest ally in the family confederacy, an extension of herself. And mothers are their daughters' role model, their biological and emotional road map, the arbiter of all their relationships." – *Victoria Secondi*

Special Dedication

Rhonda Dunn and Lori Weaver

A good teacher is like a candle. It consumes itself to light the way for others.

—Mustafa Kemal Atatürk

My dedication is given to some very special women at Learn to Read in St. Johns County, and there is special place in my heart for Rhonda Dunn.

She encourages me to complete tasks and relearning the applications of applying math and English skills to achieve the completion of reaching my GED goal, and she has inspired me to gain confidence with teamwork as it is one of the essentials for success and achieving things in this life.

I am so honored to have met her back in 2016. She has given me the courage to stand within the simplest things like applying laughter to my education, and she responds with a genuine love for learning and helping individuals grow and prosper through accepting life's challenges and conquering them one task at a time.

I realized that even a small gesture of volunteering can help someone gain wisdom to rise above any challenge in life. This one gesture helped me realize my own potential of volunteering somewhere in my own town and reaping the rewards that I can give to someone else even if it is for an hour a day.

This inspiration of her teaching and volunteering gave me the blessings of her gifts, and it inspired me to write my own story and share it with the world so that maybe one day someone could rise above and learn from my own challenges in life and give them an opportunity of inspiration or growth in their own life.

My gratitude goes along way for the special gifts given to me and all my blessings that is sustained every day after accepting the challenges in front of me.

Elaine Josephine Samella

The deep desire for adventure began as a seed and grew into your heart, as time stood still and the growth was admired of the little girl inside of you. The gift of loving animals is the gentleness conveyed around all of us. You're a cherished memory!

A daughter is a mother's gender partner, her closest ally in the family confederacy, an extension of herself. And mothers are their daughters' role model, their biological and emotional road map, the arbiter of all their relationships.

—Victoria Secondi

Mom

I loved the way, you touched my heart, as
a child and gave with no hesitation.
I loved the way, your gentleness reminded
of the flower petals spread open.
I loved the way your hand touched my little
child's hand and gave me warmth.
I loved the way, you were so sensitive to
my needs and giving with no reason.
There are no words to describe the
gift of love you gave to me.
Every year, since you have been gone
My love for you has never diminished
and I will love you for all eternity.
I will always cherish the vital moments
of love in memories of you.
Thank you, for sharing your soul
with me, as a child and teen.

Lori Weaver

Contents

Preface

The Blessings of a mother's love guides the weakest characteristics within the child and responds with admirable strength to enrich the blood and help keep the spine and bones straight and true as the soul shifts into a daughter. The gifts bestowed upon a daughter is the richness of the blood that runs deep within the imagination of the connection. This deep connection, as mother and daughter, is the serenity of bliss and the sweetest love one could ever experience as a woman.

—Dana Gregory

The gentleness from a mother's love is the foundation of learning the wisdom of nurturing within and without, but it also helps shape the real character of sensing and feeling within the soul.

The soul's expression is the everlasting footprints of the mother and daughter's legacy of the blessings unfolded between the two of them. This legacy is based upon the challenges one faced and even conquered as the other one embraces the gentleness of the surrender in deep loving ways within.

These challenges can be an extreme jump for one, but for the other one, she must sacrifice for the success to complete the rotation of the sweet and genuine love between the two of them.

This is a strong bond that builds as the mother and daughter reside with one another from birth until adulthood. It holds the emotions of strength and charisma as the daughter grows into her own identity of what she believes is grand love within, and it can help restore the balance of the earthly blessings being given back to them. They both can teach and learn from one another as the relationship grows over time.

Each one of them must define the path of love and what it means to them. The growth can either inspire or destroy the grand path of living to love within but have separate identities of passion and imagination but have one common goal in place, and that is to bring a stronger love on this earth planet.

Sometimes these challenges can have major breaking points in the growing periods and learning new information from their own paths. This gives them a stronger character to build behind what the other one has achieved by the lessons taken in and mastered.

Even as a whole experience, if these lessons were not mastered from one or the other, it always comes back from the angle of gentleness or destruction as one leaves the footprints that was walked along the journey. But if the soul refused to learn and accept love from a different point of view, the other one must take on this lesson and the deep reasons of the beginning lessons about loving within and without as a human being. The surrender of this challenge must come in stronger form and from the nurturing side and must respond with a more loving hand and even expression of highlighted words of wisdom and give to someone else this gift.

It can be softer or enlightened through the angle of a higher love that one can seek on this life experience. It can give a daughter riches in a life of love and power, but if the power is in the angle to destroy, the darker the lesson must come between the two of them.

Love is a very strong power, and if one tends to destroy such a power, it creates an imbalance of feeling unworthy and even selfish behaviors that can destroy things along the path of growth inside the quality of the character, but what I found is that there must be a present of love somewhere for the daughter and mother to survive this battle of the given path of what a woman is given here on earth, and that is to love within first and then love without to others—this strong love that was once the greatest love of all—and that is to love deeply within one another.

Life is given with such power to love and to love one another, but this life seems to have forgotten the balance of what love really means to them.

Love can build so many wonderful creations and also surrender with power by giving through healthy values. Somehow there was a breaking point with a partnership of love between a mother and daughter's love as time went on.

I can see and feel it on an extreme level, and it hurts me internally when I see families that had great love from their own mothers turn so ugly and want to destroy life.

All I ever wanted was to give all the love in the world to as many as I could, but life threw me into a hole and as I am trying to dig my way out of this hardship of lessons as I have had to face many hard lessons growing from love.

I have begun to grow into a higher love, but just like a flower, it is built from the strategy of forming and takes time to grow and blossom in the wind and fly across the skies.

This growth is the imbalance and balance of my own love journey with my mother and myself. It's had many struggles and challenges that I had to rise above and am still rising above them.

I am giving the grand opening of my life to help or guide someone in a gentle way through the expression of my story and even the growth of loving in such deep ways as I had to overcome losing a love bond with my own mother and the brief journey I shared with her but even with the blessing of learning to love again.

Elaine Josephine Samella

Born: October 23, 1939
Died: September 28, 1978

Elaine's Name Meaning

The name *Elaine* is derived from Greek, and the origin of the name meaning comes from "sun ray or shining one." It is a French variant of *Helen*. In King Arthur's myths, Elaine is a character who fell in love with Lancelot. Tennyson's poetry *Idylls of the King* may have promoted nineteenth-century revival of the name.

Behind the history of the name

The meaning and history are the gender of a feminine, and the usage is from the English Arthurian romance.

From the old French form of *Helen*. It appears in Arthurian legend, Thomas Malory's fifteenth-century compilation *Le Morte d'Arthur*.

Elaine was the daughter of Pellos, the lover of Lancelot and the mother of Galahad. It was not commonly used as an English given name until after the appearance of Tennyson's Arthurian epic, *Idylls of the King* (1859).

Elaine's meaning through the Arthurian legend was the mother to Sir Lancelot's son Galahad.

French meaning of *Elaine* is "shining one," an Old French form of Helen. The Greek meaning behind *Elaine* is "shining light" or "the bright one."

Urban Dictionary name meaning for *Elaine* is "perfect." She likes to hang out with friends and play sports. She is intelligent, loyal, and pretty. She has a great sense of humor and is semipopular.

Elaine's meaning is "a beautiful, sweet lady, and loving to all she meets." Elaines are there to hold their own if needed, morally inclined but not judgmental.

She helps others at their lowest points in life and very giving in many ways, able to deal with pain and suffering better than others.

Elaine has taken in every stray in the neighborhood in which is for the animal care—the gentleness of loving the nature and the peace that comes with taking care of things.

Elaine's Numerology

Elaine's expression number one: People with this name tend to initiate events, to be leaders rather than followers, with powerful personalities.

They tend to be focused on specific goals, experience a wealth of creative new ideas, and have the ability to implement these ideas with efficiencies and determination.

They tend to be courageous and sometimes aggressive as unique, creative individuals. They tend to resent authority and sometimes to be stubborn, proud, and impatient.

Soul urge number two: People with this name, *Elaine*, have a deep inner desire for love and companionship and want to work with others to achieve peace and harmony.

Acknowledgments

The strong bond of friendship is not always a balanced equation; friendship is not always about giving and taking in equal shares. Instead, friendship is grounded in a feeling that you know exactly who will be there for you when you need something, no matter what or when.

—Simon Sine

The journey of understanding the role one must play in any given situation is a major challenge even when matched with a deep love and friendship. It's the gaining of honesty within a true friendship, and this friendship first must come within before any other friendship can begin outside the original source of the soul.

This is the expression of the original design of acknowledging people in front of you when the sting of rejection hits the soul and self-love is gone within, but it is shared on a deep angle of loss and grieving. This is the healthiest friendship within the hurdles of moving forward in life.

It is knowing one day you can love someone, and the next day they are gone in your life. I have learned you must share your deepest thoughts to the people that love you back in this life because you never know when that day may come, and the words were not expressed to their soul and then *poof!*—they are gone forever in your life, so there is a deep need to share my thoughts and gratitude toward the people who guided my hand in my life.

My deepest satisfaction and appreciation goes toward Dana and all that she has given unto me and helping me along my journey with her. She is my best friend, but also, I deeply love her as a mother figure. I cherish the growth that she has conquered in her life but also the deep admiration for pushing me when I could not see anything in my life. She has given me a passion to go forward, and she inspires the deep honesty within me and maintaining the deep values of what I needed to become in life. I lean toward her for many answers, and she is always there giving me the support and love through it all.

My dad is the one most supportive men in my life today, and I would like to start off by saying, "Thank you for this incredible gift of love from your heart to mine." I would like to say, "This is a special gift of love that will never be forgotten, and I will always cherish it for the rest of my life."

This precious gift has made me realize the facets of love in an art form and a decision of the heart to put another person's interests above your own, and that is what you did as you gave me this gift. I have also needed and wanted to say thank you for taking such good care of me and giving me the gifts throughout the years.

I know that there have been many times where my words and actions have been insensitive. I have a hard time expressing myself. However, I want you to know that I truly appreciate from the bottom of my heart all that you have done as a father.

I personally want to say thank you for supporting me, encouraging me to follow my dreams, and even guiding me to be the best that I can be in life, but most of all is that my heart has grown fonder and even closer to you throughout the years. I am truly grateful to have a wonderful father like you, and each day that passes by, I need you to understand that I am growing stronger into the person that I am because you have lifted and made me feel very special to be a daughter of yours. I want you to know that you are my first love and hero in my life, and I will always have the deep memories that have created our father-daughter relationship with one another. Thank you for everything!

My solitude and deep passion go toward my husband and the many ingredients that he provides for me. He has always said, "Honey, I am your peanut butter and you are my jam and we stick together through it all," and we have grown closer in a more defined love as the years have passed.

There are many character traits within him that create an everlasting loving feeling inside of me, and even I have had to grow and become strong with his tender ways of teaching me. I can say this, my darling, there is no battle that I can't face without your genuine love at my core center and faith in the completion from God.

This is my deep passion within our marriage. I thank you for all that you have done for me and for all the things we will still achieve with one another as the time passes. I thank you for all those special moments that we share with one another when no one is around.

It is those quiet times that I cherish. It helps me along my journey when I get those special times with you. It reminds me of a sweet and endearing long-lasting friendship.

I can honestly say, "Life with you is everlasting." I also want you to know you are my "knight in shining armor" and that every girl dreams about. I am so honored to have found you and even still love you from this very moment in time.

This is a special thank-you for a very special animal, and his name is "Buddy." My life wasn't complete until I met his very precious soul. He has been with me through the thick and thin, and he turns around and cuddles with me even at my deepest depression stages.

He gives the utter joy of loving within and shows the extreme power of loyalty. He has given all the right things when I needed them the most in my life. He is a very beautiful character, and everyone cherishes his beautiful love because he is a bundle of happiness and love.

Another direction in a special appreciation goes toward my husband's children and grandchildren. My heart has learned a new vital role as a mother and grandmother. It has given me courage, compassion, and even wisdom from rediscovering the genuine characters that they are inside and out.

These five children of my husbands and their precious children have helped shaped my life, so I wanted to personally give them all a deep appreciation toward my growth in life. I can't express all that they have done for me.

Johanna is a very gifted and talented woman who is very loving, caring, and compassionate with others. She has been a strong and sensitive person toward the emotional challenges that I have overcome through the years.

I admire the beauty and inspirational journey that she has risen into in this life.

She has two beautiful children named Angelina and Carter, who are the most precious gifts in life because I have learned how to deeply love from a grandmother's point of view. Just watching them grow and blossom into their own characters gives me such a grand pleasure of love. They enrich the glory of living as I watch them explore and discover the world through their eyes. I thank them all for giving me this chance in life to be able to freely love and learn the quality of giving through all the hardships of love.

Jessica is a very talented woman who expresses a unique gift in which she can stand with strength and admiration from a strong loving side but also can be bold and daring when she should be. I have learned a great deal of wisdom from her and the strength that she possesses within her.

She has a sensitive side as well. She builds the strength so she can express this through her compassion to help others. She is becoming a nurse, and her character can stand with those on whom she helps along her journey.

She has two children named Emmy and Zachariah. These two are very special prizes of joy as well as my other two grandchildren. They all give me a grand feeling and the most happiness one could take in a life. They make me smile and laugh. I can honestly say, "I miss them when they are not around." What can I say—I deeply love my grandchildren!

Jeramiah is a remarkable son, and his own gift is a very strong-willed and a determined character but also compassionate and even sensitive at times. He has given me the chance to learn and embrace from his eyes on how to build my own character.

I can honestly express the defining line that makes our relationship unique. He has a special trait that gives me a feeling of protection and love like a son should give to a stepmother figure. I just wanted to thank him for all he has shared along our journey with one another.

Justin is another remarkable son, and his own character represents a sensitive, sweet, and kind soul that sparks creative thinking and believing within the shape of love. He is unique in the challenges that he faces and reaches above and beyond, and certain times he stands with abundance of compassion. He has a spin in the righteous truth and justice. I thank him for just believing in me and wanting me to become more, but he wants to see success from me, and I think from the journey with him. He has taught me a great deal about justice and seeing through the most difficult things in life. I truly always want the best for him and his life.

Josiah is another very genuine and remarkable son. He has a real and tender side to him, and he has a willing soul that softly touches your own soul. He reminds me of my own brother and the way he is very soulful.

He has a guiding hand with a sense of knowing how to embrace any situation. I am thankful for the memories and things we have shared along our journey together. Thank you for the blessings of giving through the sweet conversations and the get-togethers with all the family.

Now Scott is my biological brother, and here is another man in my life that stands out because he carries a sweet and remarkable trait of a deep inner desire for a stable loving family. His devotion toward the stability and balance gives him a unique trait of honor and compassion like no other. I admire the tender moments we shared growing up, and this has given me a deep closeness in my life. I thank him for all he has done for me, and even just the conversations give me such a calmness.

I will always treasure the deep bond that we share with one another. Thank you for always being there when I need you the most. I believe Janet has been another strength for my brother after he married her. I thank her for the joy of getting to know her as well. She has also been there for my brother but also the overall love inside of the family. I truly believe the two of them have a deep bond based in trust and love.

I also want to give thanks and appreciation to Linda, who is my father's wife. She is a very strong woman and loving toward my father. The bond between my father and her is a unique and loving journey, and I appreciate the closeness of their relationship. Thank you for loving my father and being on his journey in life.

Rhonda is a unique and strong-willed individual, but she has a deep prize of loyalty and compassion toward her friendships that are formed. My relationship with her has been a deep close bond, and she has uplifted me but also been there like a mother figure to me. I can honestly say that I truly respect her and the love she gives out to me and to others. I am thankful for her in my life. I can truly say, "There is a special bond between us."

I am grateful for the precious gifts of her soul and the wisdom she conveys to me as I have grown into a woman by the honest tenderness of her communication skills. I admire and love the deep bond we share with one another.

My deep appreciation comes from my loved ones that are no longer with me but also the ones that are in my life. These special people are my grandparents Anne and Joe.

I truly did love them with all my heart and soul. I wish they were here to enjoy reading my new book and seeing my accomplishments; I can see them and share and express my love to them. I recall that my grandmother Ann told me to go to church so that I will find someone and fall in love with for the rest of my life. I did finally go, and then I truly found my life partner. I am so glad that I did listen to her because now I am being loved in my life.

My uncle Jim is a unique and inspirational person to be around, and his wife, Ann (which is my mother's sister), helped me grow and taught me how to love.

I am very thankful for the gifts of love from them and the deep wisdom of learning in my life. I had many challenges to face, and they were there giving me their love. This inspired me to grow from a different point of view.

Also, my aunt Elisa, Pat, Rachel, and uncle Carol were all very loving toward me, and I can say that I truly loved them very much. I cherished everyone from a different angle and deeply loved them all.

Dianna and Steve are my church family at Anastasia Baptist Church, and I am very grateful to have met them. They are good friends, and I am truly blessed to have found their beautiful traits and characters.

They remind me about this Bible verse in Proverbs 19–20: "Listen to advice and accept discipline, and at the end, you will be counted among the wise." I have learned a great deal from them, and I am honored to have known their love.

Another focus on my church friends and the deep appreciation goes toward Jackie, David, and Momma Bliss. I have admired their beautiful souls and love given to me from them.

The blessings of sharing with them have been a huge part of my life, and I am thankful for all of them. Each one has a special contribution toward my healing and growing into a woman. I deeply love David's mother because she has the most divine love within her. I cherish the worship that we had at her house and the friendships that have grown overtime.

There has been a long bond of friendships through the churches within my life, and these are the people who resonated with me. They are Ed, who is very friendly; Al, who is very nice; Robert, who is unique; Betty, who is another sweet soul; and lastly Rose, who has a warm heart and is very inviting to be around. All of them have helped me during my long journey of becoming one and loving inside and out of myself.

My pastor Jerry is a very special man and very gifted in giving the messages from the Bible through him from God and then unto me. I cherish these moments of learning and growing deeper in my spiritual self, and I am honored to give my special appreciation to him. I thank you for all that you have given me along my journey.

To my dearest friendships: Sherry has been there through thick and thin and helped me grow into a stronger source of the female love. She has the purest sense of love and gives me a deep feeling of inspiration even when I was at my lowest point. She has always been a strong character that I could also look up to as a mother figure. She gives me a tender feeling of helping me to nurture the love within me.

Jim and Helen are my neighbors, and they are very sweet and intelligent, but also they give me a great sense of humor, and I have used the laughter as a tool into guiding myself into another person outside of the pain. I have learned to overcome my pain through humor, and it helps to uplift the soul into more positive energy.

Rose is another neighbor that has been a growing experience, and the deep connection of communication has built me up even stronger. She is a very kind and warm-hearted person and a great walking-around-the-block-with buddy. She became a real close friend in my life. I am honored and thankful for her in my life and also conveniently lives on my street.

Doreen is another friend that I would like to express my appreciation and love toward.

Maria was a school friend, and I wanted to express the gratitude toward our friendship and level in which I was growing and learning in my life. I am thankful for you and the love you have shown to me.

All these people have given me the chance to have known them and the opportunity to develop a satisfying, deep, and close friendships. I think my journey would not have been complete without them all because they all helped shape and guide me into a higher spiritual person. I am truly honored and wiser to have met them all in my life.

A Letter to My Dad

Dear Dad,

On the occasion of this recent gift, I would like to start off by saying thank you for this incredible gift of love from your heart to mine. I would like to say, "This is a special gift that will never be forgotten, and I will always cherish it for the rest of my life."

This precious gift has made me realize the facets of love are an attitude and a decision of the heart to put another person's interests above your own, and that is what you did as you gave me this gift.

This is not all the reasons why I am writing you this letter. I have also needed and wanted to say thank you for taking such good care of me and showing me your love throughout my life.

I know that there have been many times where my words and actions have been insensitive. I have a hard time expressing myself. However, I want you to know that I truly appreciate, from the bottom of my heart, all you have done as a father.

I personally want to say thank you for supporting me, encouraging me to follow my dreams, and even guiding me to be the best that I can be in life, but most of all, that my heart has grown fonder and even closer to you throughout the years.

I am truly grateful to have a wonderful father like you, and each day that passes by, I need you to understand that I am growing stronger into the person that I am because you have lifted me up and made me feel very special to be a daughter of yours.

I want you to know that you are my first love and hero in my life, and I will always have the deep memories that have created our father-daughter relationship with one another. Thank you for everything!

With all my love,
Lori

Lori Weaver, five months old

Gentle into the night, as a bird sings in the Harmony of love, hours pass by, and I see the footprints being left by my mother from the inside of her heart to mine.

—Dana Gregory

Lori's Name Meaning

The name *Lori* is an English baby name. In English, the meaning of the name *Lori* is "the laurel tree" or "sweet bay tree" symbolic of honor and victory, an old name with many variants.

In the Old Greek, the meaning of the name *Lori* is also known as "mercy, pity," but also in a positive direction name, meaning it is known as "bright one, shining one."

In Latin, the meaning of the name *Lori* represents a flower, blooming.

In Spanish, the meaning of the name *Lori* is "pain."

The name meaning behind *Lori* in Arabic is also known as "God is my light."

Lori has its origins in Latin and Old French techniques.

In addition, *Lori* is a diminutive (English) of Laura.

Lori is also a derivative of Spanish, Italian, Russian, English, German, and Slavic.

Lori is unusual as a baby name. Its usage peaked in 1963 with 1,203 percent of baby girls being named Lori. It had a ranking of number eight within that year; however, the baby name has experienced a substantial drop in frequencies.

What does a "laurel tree" represent?

In the myth, the god Apollo pursued Daphne in what would be interpreted today as a sexual attack. Daphne called to the river god for help and was transformed into a laurel tree—symbol of victory and triumph. The Laurel Centre represents the transformation and triumph of its clients.

Laurel is one of few plants mentioned solely in the New Testament. James suggests a laurel crown for those who preserve. Laurel is also known as shrub or small tree with evergreen, leathery leaves. Like its relative sassafras, laurel is perfused with an aromatic oil.

In the *Urban Dictionary*, the name meaning is recognized as "beautiful, smart, and funny." She is also known for her character to be the most wonderful person in the world, kind, caring, gentle, perfect in every way, and the one you will love for life.

Lori is very caring, creative, and loyal, always the best listener. She will give you sound advice but often being guilty of not taking her own good advice, not quick to trust or open up to new people; but once she's left you into her heart, you will always have a place there—provided you don't screw it up. The love to be laughing though stress rules her life. She loves to love and be loved in return. She always tries to be nice.

The one thing about Lori is when she has wild hair, she is very clever at getting the desires met. She is down-to-earth, but when pushed around, she willows away from the stress and hides her insecurity of needing to be loved and admired.

Lori is a masculine but is driven with feminine sold nature of love and how to maintain the sense of love for all in life.

Lori's Numerology

Let's first discuss the elements of what numbers mean in direction of numerology and what connection it has with the importance with any name and birthdate.

Numbers are the unique sign in the universe. Everything consists within a conception within numbers and codes.

The numerology is any belief in the divine or mystical relationship between a number and one or more coinciding events. It is also a study of the numerical value of the letters in words, names, dates, and ideas. It is also alongside or associated with the paranormal and astrology and similar divinatory arts.

Let's break down the numbers in the name *Lori*. The letter *L* is the number 13 and the *O* is represented as the number 16 and *R* is associated with the number 19 and *I* is, again, the number 9, so when you add these altogether—1+3+1+6+1+9+9=30— and then add 3+0=3, and there you have the numerology of the name *Lori* broken down from the alphabet and the numbers connected to the letters.

This helps an individual to understand the depths from the inside of themselves from the level of God because he created all of us.

The number 3 in name meaning contributes and guides to the inner soul of understanding of the name and number system which has great value in life.

The 3 represents the half of the number 8, and it is constantly looking for ways to improve; however, it is different than 1 and 2 because the number 3 is very restless and moveable—playful, creative, constantly receiving, giving, and playing as a child.

Jupiter rules number 3 and so the planet is a very big planet and so this has an eye for big things and a life of luxury, positive and wise, delicate, but you do not dig deeper into the finer things that will help the inner character rise up and take the risks needed, but outflow shows the buildup of frustrations and resentments of not creating your destiny in front of you.

You like to live in the moment and are in constant change around you, but this internal frightens the number 3's and yet scales back the deep inner leader of a playful child.

You and even craft things very quickly and number 3 that tends to not like to plan things, but you like to be optimistic.

If number 3's find things very taxing, then they change the direction and then get into something else, living in the moment and getting those of fun.

This is a very hard conflict when not diving into the details of things like going internal and understanding the depths of a finer and core complexity component of the inner self, but once the 3's get a handle of this work, they can achieve the levels of the unknown from a unique perspective in which no one had seen before.

The number 3's are nonpressured cohabitual people, and when pressure hits, then the insecurity runs the roadmap in front of them. You like to be free of pressure and also like the easy way at all cost. However, the number 3's do have a low resistance in responsibilities; but when nurtured about how to take on the pressure and handle the stress, then the kindness and compassion comes out in handfuls.

The number 3's take the path of the easy road because you do not like confrontations, and you are not like the number 2's, which have the diplomatic side—the side of less pressure rings true for the 3's.

Jupiter makes you very loyal and honest.

The number 3's like to express through words or actions, do not like to do the research that is necessary, but they would become great writers and painters and artists.

Share with the others.

There are some difficulties with number 3's because they lack the confidence in achieving because they are on a sole basis of needing change of the environment.

Birth calculations numerology

The birth calculation means you are adding your birth numbers to signal digit to get to the life lesson and/or vibration or frequencies.

Lori's birthdate is 02-25-1963, so when you calculate 2+2+5+1+9+6+3=28, and so again, adding the numbers to a signal digit. Add 2+8=10 and then again add 1+0= 1, so now that we have a signal digit of a number, this is where the number means something in the numerology system.

The number one represents "a leader," someone who makes a dent in the world from the inner knowledge of growth because they have known defeat, known loss, and have struggled and have found their way out of the depths and into a beautiful leader, then you have a known individual with running ground.

They can make a difference in the world because this person has had the appreciation and sensitivity and an understanding of life and the passion fulfillment of the deepest compassion, gentleness, and a deep loving nature that make something happen in the world.

The internal world of knowing what it is really like from the inside out and outside being stuck in a negative reality—that does not work and can change what needs to be done here on earth from the perspective of God and the inner power of working through to make the change.

The number 1's need a focus and direction placed with them, and then they can in surrogate the process in which they were plainly stuck in and when they can reach the destiny through means of understanding the great path that lies in front of them.

The number 1 is a primal force—creativity, new beginnings, purity of purpose, the leader, determination, the great warrior, honor and responsibilities, the inflated ego.

So when the number 1's are engaged with the ego and selfish side, it's running the show which creates the roadblocks come not by not confronting the ego and/or inflating the ego. This is when challenges rise in an unhealthy manner, which also causes more stress and even more added pressure to the number 1's.

On the basis of the number 1's, if the ego is inflated and comes back down to earth, it becomes a more well-rounded individual. This is when the leader can shine the bright light of the soul.

Character of the body is number 1, and it shows the high self-esteem and are highly realistic, and you have your own way of your own mind. You also portray and listen to your mind.

You are a very active and enthusiastic but eager driven, and you like new things too. You like to be creative and creating new things and the overall balance of starting new things.

The domination to make your goals to become successful in creating is sometimes difficult when this is when the stubbornness takes the road map and breaks down the process through the full flesh of responsibilities because the stubbornness side lacks in taking on the end results of the projects which in the turns to frustrations toward the number 1's.

The best stages for the number 1's is to maintain the challenge and see it through all the stages of new beginnings into the final results.

Special Poems

Beauty

Beauty lies within your soul
It's comfortable to know
That it can overflow the bowl,
If you personally forget:
There is always someone there
To give you a lift
And show you again,
That there still is
Beauty within.

Pain

I can't breathe
Inside this cold breeze
That passes by
Because everything I do
Is lie
And freeze up inside
For I hold no boundaries
If I can't cry
It all traps me.

A Glass Mirror

I whisper colors inside my ear:
Impulse of hidden tears,
Reflections within a glass mirror
A spiral of fears
Drain into the glass mirror;
Open-water doors
Steer away
A fragile deer
Out of the glass mirror

Loss

I can't think anymore—I used to be able to think,
I can't cry anymore—I used to be able to cry,
I feel empty all the time—I used to feel full,
I'm tired all the time—I used to
have all kinds of energy,
I think everything is my fault—I
used to know that it wasn't,
I don't feel things anymore—I used to feel shocked
I won't tell myself what I am feeling—
I used to share my feelings with my friends
I'm a stranger to myself
I've lost me

I Wanted

I stood holding onto something
That touched my heart and soul
When I reached in, I felt nothing
And had no choice but to let it go
In life that's all I wanted
Was something "To fill -my hole."

Mother

I see you
And
Feel you
Through a baby's
Tear drops
Holding me so dear
I see you and feel you
Inside the warm
Weather
Holding onto me as
A feather,
I see you and feel you
Holding onto a
beautiful flower
It reflects to each moment
Of love

The Connection of Loss

Within a mirror track of moments of
Emptiness not fates
A Flight Home
A feather dance within—
Beautiful dreams bend
Collides inside movements
Of Light
Strange but true
A white dove
Glides
A soul back home
Inside a love flight home

Vital Reds

Breathing flowers
Turn my mother
Into a golden shower
In the midst, of a rainforest
My mother turns inward
And raises her eyebrows
In a desire of fate.
A moment of pleasure turns
Back to faith and back
Again, to deceit.
The connection of loss
Within a mirror track
Of moments of- Emptiness
And the cloths
Deepens in the soul
And wonders of the night glow
Of the sadness left but bestowed
Upon the love found
Of a vital red flower

A Flight Home

A feather dance within
Beautiful dreams bend
Collides inside movements
Of flight.
Strange but true
A white dove glides
A soul back home
Inside a love flight home.
Combination
But dreams
Of a soul
Lost without a flight home
Glory to the flowers
Of whiskers edge
Of my love beckons
Within
I cherish
The love of life
As I am seen
With your flight
I stand within you
And stand behind you
Forever flight

Tears

Tears—they come and go
Knowledge is there to know
And show people
How to grow
It's a key
To understand why our systems
Live in and embrace the pain

A Lover's Journey

Intimacy
Touch
And loneliness
When do they meet?
A clock
A duck
And a wall
The man says, "Take a seat"
She turns towards him
And believes
Is this love
Or defeat
She gains wisdom
As the growth shines
Breaking codes
Of all there was within
Now the journey begins
Silhouette of white
Glows and dimes
Passion arises
And sets
Awhile the glory is waited upon
Evening grows

As the winds blow
Each waking step leads
And ends with just opening
With the deepest love
One could find in life

Breaking the Bondage of Trust

Sickles of icicles are formed around the soul
When the soul begins to form a
frame of mind of trust
The bondage of love is the
beginning stages of this trust
The sensations that grow within this form
Begin to be shaped and curved
around the blessings of the soul
The sentiments of values are twisted
into the curve of other planets
This curve resonates only due to the
source of the value of the universe
But this source is unvalued within
the core of this planet
The destruction of living under
a non-heavenly reality
Means the taste of love is without and not within
The bondage of this is the source of the cycle
Breakage of this cycle means
Tampering within the values of the physical desires
Into the soul's heavenly bounce back into life
The uneven balance creates dysfunctions
and a cloudy like form within the mind

The eye can't see the reality around them,
but the reality of the vision created
This vision is bounced in and out of the values
of your core and the simple joys in life
So, how does one begin the stages of
breakage of such source of un-reality
When the reality of values is formed
Around the soul's core within values.
The bondage of sexual creation
within trust is the key
To break all bondage of these values
Digging within to the breakage of the
source of the bondage of trust
Knowing where in location is my own split
Balancing within values but breakage
of unreality of values
This is when the values of sex are
correlated into a reality
When is the most functional state of being?
Creation is being formed around the
dysfunctional state of being.
It's when the soul realizes that
creation is the form of a split
You see when you form your mind around
the split with sex and relationships
You are disconnected to the soul
Shaping the reality of what we
think is within our society
Shaping relationships around creation energy and
the second brain around dysfunctional values
These values are based on the second brain

A CALL TOWARDS LOVE

Inside of your sexuality energy and gravity
Within the lives of our souls
Now seeing where the location is at base of the soul
Now reconnecting
Is the hardest part
Digging and digging is base within the base
Of the unreality check of instilled
in values of the core
This is at the functional state of the
mother and the program
When you bond with the mother and
bondage formed is based on the same
Dysfunctional state of mind, then the soul is
Bonded with the mother and the soul's path
So, the trust was formed within the core of
The mother and father in which states the
Soul can have multiple splits within the soul
That were formed within the value system
So, when the form of trust and bondage is
The connection the core of the
original source and the parents.
So, to break this bondage of this love means
You must break off the love within the
Parents first and then open to the
love within of heavenly soul
This is when the source begins to break
Down the core values of the
dysfunctional state of mind
So, when the mind is still split, then one
Must dig at the core of the unreality
of what is and is not

Split system is the major function at
which the world revolves around.
Everything must be split up to
have devious outcomes
Therefore, the outcome of reality is unbalanced
Splitting the soul with sex means
controlling through the split
The soul has no way out when the soul
Only sees sex
And not created values within
values inside of our soul
This is how the outcome of the government
is splitting the whole into divine
For themselves
Taking the soul's purpose and the money
flow in which governs that source
Is the place on which they stand within?
This is when you see the core of their
values and not your own.
Awakened
Now you can see the base value in
which they split the system
Access to N eo-cheating of money
and low integrity of the system
And the bondage of what is at the core of reality
Stealing the source of your soul and
Purpose is the bondage of trust they desire
But the desire in your soul is to accomplish
The values in which you wanted to
create for your life and others.
This is the unbalance in which they create for power

A CALL TOWARDS LOVE

It's stealing power from you by splitting the
Source of your own values within their own
Dysfunctional state of values which is based
On sex and gravity within the body flow
And so, this flow is then stirred back them
Because they are stealing the flow
for money and power.
So, the ones holding the Icon state
Is also in the alignment of stealing for
Power
The values they are holding is
based on sex and power.
It's not dignified but created to form the
Reality check of the world.
Getting enough numbers of humans to believe
In such trash of reality is the game of rush
And then source is planted within the mind set
And then values are then formed about sex
Then relationships are destroyed by rage
Because the anger is based on the value structure
Against the soul and creating values of a whole
The unity is broken and money flows
This how you see the check reality
in the game of chess
You can see the reality
And you open your eyes in another way of life.
Therefore, they close the perceptions within you
To keep the flow going.
The journey inward
Trust is the key in which the soul travels on

With this is the ultimate source
in which holds the soul
The trust battle is gaining access within the sources
Rather it be stealing information
or gathering information
This is the base in which the human
soul cannot balance within
The soul's unit system is based on trust
And when the soul mistrusts the core of oneself
Then, the soul is faced with non-
attachments within a source
The soul resides in the gravity field and sexual arena
Because the soul has no trust within
the core of the beliefs of the who
And/or what is within.
The soul is faced with uncertainty
And the glory stands within of others.
This is when the values need to be faced of
what was back then and what is now
For the honesty to set in
When the system is circulating around you
There is a locked system within the
core and cannot be broken
Unless there is one value that is broken,
This one value
You must find and re-circle the information
To gain access to higher self
The balance is the core
The core is the value.
So, what is the core within the
gravity field and sexuality

A CALL TOWARDS LOVE

I see control, and attention but is this
it or does it go deeper than this
Is this the key
The gravity field holds karma
Karma is a universal thing and
when holding this karma
One has control and attention
However, there is more than this of course
Because the key elements control the base of trust
What is the thing to find?
In order to break the damage of the trust
And locate the door in which trust has been broken
This broken door is the location in
which all shields hold against
With the balance of trust.
This door has many splendors of the nights
And challenges the base of what is
the truth and what is the lie.
This is when life can begin
When the soul locates the core of
those values within trust
And break down the whole system
and launch forward.
This is balance of the game in
which the source is within
Find the hidden secret and gem
and there you have the key
Of all split

A Daughter's Love

A climb into the world without a wing
Freshness stops with time
As the breath takes
A moment to break free of the one she loved
So effortlessly
And yet!
Time sneaks away
Forever the flower of thorns
Gone—But a forever song
Was built within the walls—Of love
Inside of a daughter's love
As she remembers the one who holds the key
Of her future
And she can dream
Without the mother
Fear is taken to extreme
As the daughter aches
So deeply
A cry of a whistle's dove
Expresses the one of purity
Within soldier of time
But aches within silence
The emotions are bogged down

A CALL TOWARDS LOVE

And yet!
She found a dream
Inside
As the daughter loves within
She awakes again!

Missing You

Defining a strolling rebelliousness within
It's surprising the gentle heart
Rainbows and storms give me a gift
However, the shivers of calling out your name
Leaves footprints from my physical self
The cuts and scrapes of the silence
Can't edge my seat in the sol's grass
Upon earth,
Emptiness and hollow doors
Define the reasons why I am here
I come to you,
To beg for the sol to return and this is the glory
I wait upon the claim of you
The gentleness and yet, the hardship
Of no return—
Of growing without you I sit within the lines
Calling the wind
And the blocks in front of me Are always there
I am sorry for not digging deeper than I was
In the mission but life wanted to know the truth so,
My life would not falter in unwanted
Passions of the unified designs-here-on-earth —
I begged for the life I wanted and then I

A CALL TOWARDS LOVE

Rejected it because of the resistance built within me,
I cry for the choices in those seconds
I cry for the blessings that will come from
The hard work again that is in front of me.
I stand within the walls of the lonely of my friend's
But I also cry for the lives n-seen of the
Visions that I dreamed
I stand with prod emotions but fall within
This stance because others have
talent and myself is broken
I am not sure what the mission is without
The soul. But what I am certain for is the
Love I had in a split second and no one
Really knows what it feels like
But I do
Calling to the staircase that I must climb back in
My own soul
It's the desire to never leave
I desired for the long hours of my soul of
My mother to love
Crying to the world
Why?
As I begged for mercy
And begging for forgiveness
For my thought un-desired in negative
I am the substance
I am the glue of my own shoes
I am the trust
And the soul's journey in front of me
But the story is still playing
Who called this story?

Did he write such a story within my mind?
Or did he keep this story playing endless over me—
I just want a life without pain
Can I want this?
For you and for me
I send memories and moments of
the heartache to myself
Because those choices
Why?
I beg and cry for nothing but I want
Something within the love of life.
Standing with life and the gifts granted unto me
Gone!
I say, "They are gone!"
No one ever knew who I was and
what I did for this life
Only me
I gave with everything
I gave without return
And I gave in the hope for life and then
I get nothing—
Maybe I should have been selfish then
Everyone would have known me and the
Sensations of my soul
And then, I share on whom I was in the moments
I wonder in my own mind would they have
Believed me or would they have taken from me.
Since we live in a cruel world.
I ask did I handle everything in the best
Way or did I make mistakes and cry for
Those moments of the mistakes.

A CALL TOWARDS LOVE

Would they have believed me on how I truly loved?
Or would they have scorned me for the way
I was taught to love which was
to lust in relationships.
And think it was love.
No one will know me but me and the
Challenge I faced but me—I look back and see
A woman growing inside the hard edge
I call for the heaven
Seek the blessings and give out to those around me
What was given unto me?
And the world scorns on what
actions they do themselves
I hopeless and crying and one day,
The world will know what I left and the
Footprints of my legacy.

Saying Goodbye

Silence:
Words are dry.
I just cry, and I say, "Oh, my!"
As you give a rose to say
Your goodbye.
With sincere grace, I fly
In the deepest sighs.
My love never dies.

Stretching Within

All the day, I cry.
Inside or outside,
Tumbles of lies
Reach a battle of cries,
Forever dreamed alive.

A Cry Out

I hear a cry so loud and yet I hear no sound
Oh, for I do not speak
In a sound
Of a lost echo
Called "A Cry Out"
From the loud cry
It's bound inside
That hits the bottom
Of the dreams
For then it's there
In a dead rose
That dies

Life

Have you ever gone through life?
Not understanding
What life really means
In depth!
You completely -Want to understand
When the words are expressed
But the emotions
Are locked away
Feelings enmeshed
Life moves on past you
And the words stay the same
It's all gathered in a form of stress
A Stranger
Gives
And all you know is to give back
All your true emotions
Then you realize
Life has passed without you
In a passion un-dressed, you cope
Without a deep understanding
Of life

The Real You!

Most people in the deep seas
Got off by making fun of me
If the world would ever be in my shoes
They would happen to see
What's truly inside of me?
And then,
Lost in wonder of whom they are inside
As the other part of them had died
Then, they would see all the reasons of the new
For their discovery of themselves
Of why I say, "You need to understand the real you!"

Human Life

All—climb the wall,
Some fall,
Others stall,
Who are you inside this cry of life?

Mother's Day

I am here in a sweet whisper
On a beautiful sunny day
As I turn inward
Of my true experience
Without my mother—
On Mother's Day
I listened to the doors
Slip into a scream
That glitters among
The sweetest dream
In May

Self-Doubt Cleanse

My journey inward
Afraid, loss
Cries, words
Built highly
In regards
to a solid
Statue
"I" Stand
Looking for the truth within
Gone
Painlessly
Awakes
The word
Doubt
"I"
Sink deeper
Inside
"I"
Feel it
Digging
And digging
For more truth
"I"

I
Surrender
To my creative
Eye
On who sees?
The honesty
Within
"I"

Emotional Eating

Lonely, stressed
Only in rewards
Leads to emotional eating
Bank forward
In a connection—to the soul
And you lose
The empty trust
That binds you—to this black hole
Gather your thoughts—own them
And surrender to self
Within child's mind

An Ugly Face

You glare at me with your eyes
And then turn back away from me
Because you only saw
An ugly face
Staring back at you
With an open heart
Full of a lingering love
Inside a genuine art

Clinging Appetite

Clothes fitted and blown
No need to sow
A father's glow
Of a morning dew
Within brightness
Of heaven's snow
I linger deeper into a dream
And sense the presence of emptiness
Lingering on—closed heart
But a full stomach

I Thank You!

I search the hours, from my life
I bottle up the only way I know
As you slowly merge in,
Each layer
If you listen, you'll see
The true reasons
Of why
I thank you!

Fresh Start

You plunder around many years
Through the fresh start
You release many hidden tears
You require a lot—for the fresh start
That you turn so desperate
Later on you fill your stomach up
With all regrets
Experience is all you need
To rush through life—with a pleasant of speed
Come to a child of the last phase
Knowing what to do
When you come to the last maze
You churn for the excitement
Oh, heart—And you at the end
That is not completely done

A Heart Full of Grief

Undo it, take it back, and make every day
reappear again
Until the day of your death
The days after I held tight within me
Forth I never wanted to let you go
In the memories of my mother's hands
What can contain this rage?
A woman, a man or neither
An armed tanker
All is lost in the explosion
When a door is closed of all emotions

Grant Me a Wish

I stand in a middle of a puddle of thin eyes
The search began to render within me
As a Farther opens the skies
The truth awakens in me
I turn to you
For you to
Grant me a wish
I ask upon you—to give a love
Those will last forever
As a man turns into a dove
Dancing above and around a feather

Love

A sweet warm energy,
Glides us to a connection
To one another,
And it will be a blessed
Emotional expression,
Inside of you and with others
When you're open to receive this
Energy connection

IF

If I had to raise my inner child again
I'd finger paint more and point the finger
less,
I'd does less correcting and more
connecting
I'd take my eyes off my watch and watch
more with my eyes
I'd care to know less and know how to care
I'd take more hikes and fly more kites
I'd stop playing serious and seriously play
I'd run through more fields and gaze at more stars
I'd do more hugging and less tugging
I'd build self-esteem first and then the house later
I'd be firm less often and affirm much more
I'd teach less about love of power and teach about
The Power of Love

Soul Life

A break into a life
Consciousness leaves you
Open to all lies
Power belongs to all shoes
Otherwise, you're stuck in muck
This is when the soul
Is blocked
But when opened
Like a flower
It spreads
All over the world.

Power of Love

Love is the thing that ties us together
It makes us breathe inside
A warm feather,
As it connects in one
Soul and others
We can release a good energy
Through one's body and mind
For the pressures come
When the heart fears
What the other causes
On a tiger's eye forms tears
When we all are not loved

Mother's Nature

A womb is full of expressed love
And gentleness from a touch
Within the eye's or words
In the mother's mind
It rebirths
Nurtures,
Creates
Our beautiful life
It also blends inside the earth and land
But we as, mothers, get to hold the life
That we created in a human form.

A Drip

Tears drip on the inside of your soul
As each day can pass
Without the touch from your mind
That skips a beat in a musical line
Which makes you—you forget the lessons
Of what can make you whole

If Only

If only I had known the difference
(Ah but you didn't)
If only I had thought
(It was not allowed)
If only I had discovered
(Choices were taken)
Why didn't I once tell you?
(Lies unfolded)
I hated you for growing stronger, and forgetting me
(I embraced myself within)
If only I had not failed you
(Wow I loved you)
If only you could forgive yourself
(Freedom appears)
I whisper and say
(If Only)

—Poems by Dana Gregory

A Call Towards Love

1

Opening the Spaces to Love

In the silence of an early spring morning, serenity calls toward my soul. It's living to love within, but the edges of living a life of emptiness without a mother's love is the insanity of breaking free from the chains that bind me. On September 28, 1976, my mother committed suicide.

It's this traumatic event that internally blocks me from truly loving myself, and even though I am in full grips of embracing the honor of my mother's love on the physical side of my own character, I felt as a child, teenager, and even as an adult, there is a hidden spiritual doorway that cannot be opened.

I struggle with this emptiness that plagues my heart in every way. However, it does feel like something is missing in my life and this feeling is the strong and natural expression of love and it comes from my mother. But there is another deep feeling of loss, and this loss occurred when I was a young teen—when my mother decided to end her life by committing suicide.

The dream of wanting to let go of the emptiness inside of me seems very far away from me, so there is a deep yearning to let go of the feeling of the emptiness with something else besides the heartache of losing my mother. But there are so many memories that made me feel important, so I feel trapped inside of my own emotions; and the outside of me feels like embracing the whole world around me, but I climb right back into my hole and surrender back to the emptiness of the loss of my mother.

The completion of this resides with the mother-daughter's relationship and my own internal will-power to overcome this cycle going inside of me. The hardest challenge is the bond between the two of us—it's a deep and complex bond which makes it the strongest energy within a relationship, and I have shaped my own relationships regarding my mother's love and my life around this complex relationship of my mother and me.

The most difficult part as a daughter without a mother is the advice in relationships and trying to move forward with my life, but I find myself riding the curb of wanting to hold on to those memories and then wanting to let go; and when the feeling comes through me as a breaking point, I feel the edges of life creeping through me, and then I can't imagine letting her go from my mind.

At certain times, I just numb myself and eat to block these extreme emotions, or there is a strong need to improve in some way; but other times, I just go through crisis moments of anger with myself or in my relationships.

When the anger comes, I can't see other people's emotions because the heat of the anger drives me to ignore things as I am in the hot sandbox and full of deep hurt, just crying out for someone to take this sword of rejection out of my heart.

I do know that there has been plenty of times that I just come to terms with what is and what isn't at certain moments in my life, but there is a hard point in my existence of just losing all insights of staying strong, and a part of me takes moments about thinking of taking my own life because I can feel the impact of my own mother's path, and so I have to fight on a constant basis on what is the most important things at this moment to drive forward in my life.

It's just the devastation of losing something so strong such as a mother's love. It is an endless searching agony and empty days of emotions with not being able to share a conversation or even standing by her to reach out and give a hug to her.

This is an internal ache within me that penetrates my whole subconscious and conscious thoughts from time to time. I just wonder if there will ever be a grand day that we will once hold one another, but my uncertainty with myself leaves me in wonder if I will ever come to peace with this traumatic event.

However, I know that I am loved, and all I wanted in my own life is happening, but I must come to terms with the now and realize this is not the honesty in front of me, so I turn inward and reach for something to feel wanted and accepted from someone outside of me.

The honesty of losing someone so important in your life takes you on different stages of growth as you learn how to cope with the loss of someone so strong in your life and you admired for a long time in the memories of my early childhood.

To know wisdom and instruction; to perceive the worlds of understanding; to receive the instructions of wisdom, justice, and judgement, and equity; to give subtility to the simple, to the young man knowledge and discretion; a wise man will hear, and increase learning; and a man of understanding shall attain unto wise counsels. (Proverbs 1:2–5)

It's this honesty that keeps the doorway clear for not following in my mother's footsteps.

I cling to the idea of asking these questions internally and even outwardly with other people that came in and out of my life.

These questions come in and out of my consciousness, and sometimes it consumes my every thought as I embrace these questions as the tears embrace me as I ask this: "Why, mother? Why did you take your own life?" The next deeper question I ask within is "What did I do as a child for you to not want to hold on and leave me in another town or even another state?

"We could have started a new life with one another, and I, as a teen, could have helped you in every way, but you didn't give me this chance to grow and help you with another deep love from a daughter's love. My love could have sustained you, and we could have gotten you some help, but I didn't even know there were so many deep issues inside of you."

It hurts me because I feel like I am not important with giving my love to people. I shy away from this experience because I feel deep within a loss, and this is the ache not being able to express to myself as well as to other people. It's a daughter's love that drives a teen into an adult, and I deeply felt that I was missing this element in my life. However, these honest memories can ease some of the agony, but it doesn't take that sharp pain away from me as I was growing as a teen and even into an adult.

Therefore, I have some delicate memories of when I was younger with my mother, and so by sharing a little bit about my experience, it gives me a little reassurance of this love that I had felt with her, and it helps me to reenact those memories for survival when life brings me down during my life's struggles.

I remember my tender moments as a child, and I recall memories of my mother giving me birthday parties at home. We invited my friends, and they would come. When I was younger, we used to always have chocolate cake with icing and candles to blow out, and that was one of the best things because I was a chocolate addict.

I would love it when my mother would even bake me a special cake for me because it made me feel even more special when I got to see the cake with candles. I would literally go internally crazy inside as though it was a famous cake and I was the legend—well, this was in my mind at the time or in the moment. I can see the parties and even some of the games that we played with one another.

My neighborhood friends would come to celebrate with me with the balloons and all the decorations hanging all around. I swear it was like Christmas, but it was dedicated just for me, and I loved it.

I remember getting presents, and we always seem to play pin the tail on the donkey and board games like Candyland and Monopoly. In good weather, the adults would shoo us outside, and we would play kick ball, jump rope, hop scotch, hide and seek, and rover, rover come right over. This was when the little girl came out and just soared in play. There was nothing that could stop me from smiling.

At one party, when I was about eight years old, I wore my favorite purple dress with flowers! I was twelve or thirteen when my mom committed suicide. I still have a tough time talking about it because the sensitive side of me creeps in and just takes over, and there I am finding myself in a puddle of mush in my room alone.

My mom was a very friendly, kind, and compassionate person, and I know people adored the gentleness of her soul. She was outgoing and loved to talk and socialize. She was about the height that I am now, about five feet four inches, and she had brown eyes. She had long brown hair, and she put it up in rollers a lot so that when she took it down and combed it, it looked pretty.

My mom liked to play tennis a couple of times a week. She dressed casually most of the time in blue jeans and shirts, but she dressed up from time to time (especially for church where we went as a family), and she always looked very pretty when she dressed up.

One thing that I really remember about her is that the perfume she really liked to wear was White Shoulders. It smelled so good, so as you can imagine, the scent of it always reminds me of my mom. I remember giving her hibiscus flowers and cards because I loved her so very much.

We had a black poodle back then named Suzy. Mom used to get Suzy's nails painted pink and put a bow in her fur! I think that got me to loving animals and especially dogs. We lived in Hialeah, Florida, for a long time. In fact, that's where we were when my mom passed.

I had a friend I grew up with in Hialeah. We're still best friends. Her name is Sherry Douglas, and her mom, Shirley, was friends with my mom because we lived on the same street. Ever since my mom passed, I've called Shirley "Mom"! When Sherry and I were young, we liked to play school and play house and jacks! We played card games like rummy and Monopoly. I always picked the little Monopoly dog to go around the board!

Sherry and I got to swim in the lake behind her house. Sherry and I did so much together, and it's hard to remember everything we did. We talked a lot about family and friends. We went to elementary and junior high together. We really didn't have classes together.

I didn't like school because I didn't excel like the other children in my class, and I always had difficulty with learning because my memory seemed off-center with irrational thoughts from time to time, but the clarity of being around other classmates seemed a bit easier than facing homework assignments in class.

Trying to balance home life and separating my own anxiety of being around other people created havoc around my ability to focus on studying and learning through school.

I enjoyed the friend even though I didn't have that many friends. At recess, we played kickball. I especially hated dressing out although I did have a crush on my junior high coach. I wasn't athletic. I just went to school and came home. I lived with my mom.

Then I lived with my grandparents, and then I lived with my dad. My mom and dad were together off and on, and they were together when my mom passed. I don't think they had much fun together. They argued some.

After my mom died, I developed posttraumatic stress disorder (PTSD). I had no idea what was going on internally, but I knew things were not going right inside of me.

I have memories about things that went on. When my dad found my mom, he sent me next door to my neighbor's house. The ambulance came and the medics took my mom away and to this day, when I'm outside and I hear sirens, I panic. It's so bad that I run inside. When I panic, I get physically tight in my body. It's a hard thing to go through.

I've done some research about PTSD, and I've learned that it affects a person's self-worth—and a person's self-worth is really the core of your identity. So I'm giving you some self-worth affirmations here for you to recite each day to help your self-esteem because kindness to yourself is associated with the area of the brain that creates positive emotions.

Some affirmations to help build more positive thoughts are "I have self-worth." "I like myself without comparing myself to others." "I can do a good work at my job." "I do my best whenever I do anything." My self-esteem affirmation for when I hear sirens is "I am brave when I hear sirens."

The Lord said "I Am" therefore:
"I Am"
So use these words wisely, for those words
have power to overcome any obstacles.
I Am Responsible for Choices.>>

Confront the dark parts of yourself and work to banish them with illumination and forgiveness. Your willingness to wrestle with your demons will cause your angels to sing.

—August Wilson

Another way that I have found to improve the core of my own self-esteem is to connect with nature because it makes me feel good. When I see beauty and watch things grow, it's nurturing for me. I also found in my research that being mindful leads to having more compassion for yourself and for others.

Being mindful means accepting yourself whether your current thoughts are right or wrong, but once I realized that I had PTSD, I realized that I need to just go on and deal with certain things.

One way that I deal with it is not to go outside a lot, but I really like to go to high school football games and I like to walk the dog and to visit my friends, and that means going out of my comfort zones.

I believe that anyone can do anything if they put their mind to it. When you are a slow learner, people think that you can't do anything, but that's not true. Over a long period of time, I have come to the conclusions that one can rebuild the mind and pick up some knowledge along the way. It is a long road of deep understanding to trusting and loving inside, but there were many days of the darkness impeding in my daily life.

My emotional self was injured through the process of not knowing why my mother committed suicide. It nagged at my heart because my family protected me from the scene, and after I went to my grandmother's house, I think the shock grew into a monster, and fear began overwhelming me from this one fateful day.

No one really knows the ache of the loss of love from a mother until the day you get this heartbreaking news that just shatters your life forever. Just hearing the words of a mother dying is a tug at me internally. My sensitive nature is drawn back to that fateful day again and again.

The day my mother made that final decision was when I was at school and my brother found her lying in the bedroom. My brother and father took over as I was sent to my grandmother's house after school.

I remember vaguely of things, but my mind was full of anger and shock at this moment but mostly feeling so lonely and afraid of never having my mother again. This was all I could think of as my grandmother was in shock as well when the devastation hit us. We cried for hours with one another.

I honestly can't recall if I even ate that day, but I know my grandmother loved to cook delicious meals, and so I remember being curled up on a bed, and my thoughts were racing on what was really going on over at my parents' house.

I believe in my mind my thoughts grasped the idea that they could save her but then as the news got worse and worse that my mother was completely gone, after hearing my grandmother saying, "Honey, it is going to be all right" and inside I wanted to believe her, the emotions could not comprehend those actual words of comfort.

The images in my head were going dark as well as the emotions deep inside of me. I just was barely focusing on breathing and then I heard the silence and then ambulance and the rescue truck with loud sirens, and I knew inside that my mother was in that ambulance and there was nothing I could do but feel so hopeless. I screamed so loud and began crying that I would never see my mother ever again.

The streams of tears seemed to never stop. The agony was going deep within me as the days passed by. I could just only react, but then family began showing up for comfort at the loss of my mother. It just kept stirring more pain as the funeral was being arranged.

Every moment of watching others mourn of the loss of my mother made me realize the shared joy of the same love that my mother had for others in her life. I got to understand my mother a little deeper and the love she gave to others. The boldness of her character and taking charge of things made me want to be just like her.

A strong memory of her that I held on internally and that was of great joy was always watching her do her own hair every morning and that she would be cleaning up after everyone, but I realized how beautiful she was and how carefree outwardly to others she became, but I did not know internally she was fighting demons of not wanting to live and the anguish she had inside of her.

I know she gave me the impression of importance on what to wear and how to behave around others. After she had left her body and after her funeral, it made it real. I just went numb inside, totally lost my identity of what she even shared with me.

She impressed and inspired me so much that I just wanted to be like her, and when I grew up, I wanted to find a man to love and become the woman that she wanted me to be in life.

Life began to turn ugly inside of me when my mother's suicide began to haunt my dreams, but I did not really pay attention to them, only when I had to face them for moments. I would internally run away from my stability and hope someone would make the pain just simply go away.

My grandmother called me one day and asked me if I wanted to come over, and I said, "I would love to, Grandma," and so she drove over and picked me up from my father's house.

My grandmother shared and read the letter to me that my mother had written in school. This gave me an ahh feeling inside, and my magic came alive again after my grandmother reached out to help me.

The hours began with Grandma helping me write out the assignment on a piece of paper, and by the time we got done with the words and expression in how to write again, it gave me the highest feeling of mastering something even when I had deep ache inside of me.

I knew life should be better on the outside, so I learned to cope with the expressions of love on the outside of me, but this day seemed a bit different than most. I felt like I was being real, and I honestly began to try harder in school.

A few months passed, and I began remembering that my mother was a great writer and so I worked endlessly for this assignment and I called my grand-mother up and asked her how she was doing, and she said, "I am cleaning the house," and I said to Grandma, "I wrote a paper for my assignment."

Grandma said, "You did? That is great news!" And so I was very insecure about how I wrote the paper and asked Grandma if I could read it to her over the phone, and Grandma said, "Yes, I would love to hear it."

After reading it to her, Grandma paused and reflected in her mind and said, "Wow, you wrote a great paper!"

She replied back again and said, "It sounded like a college paper and that it was very impressive."

I could not believe my grandmother said, "You're going to get an A plus from that paper."

I said, "You think so, Grandmother?" and she sighed for a moment and said, "Yes, my darling. You did an awesome paper!"

I turned inwardly as my grandmother kept praising me for the hard work and dedication inside of the assignment.

Later assignments began to get harder and harder as each time I began to reflect to my grandmother reading that letter and how it touched me so deeply. This helped me, but it also shined the light inside of the emotional side of my mother passing.

Sentimental and emotional bonding with life and learning to love as a teenager. I was happy on the outside and getting a picture with my dog. The swing set helped me play again.

Mother and daughter's bond

2

The Depression Strangles Me

The entanglement of the heaviness of the emotions from my mother committing suicide seemed as it was never going to end. The engulfment of the energy from a sensitive level and an intuitive side of me began echoing the silence, and then deafness inside of me began to turn off to the death, and yes, years passed, but I calmly had to register for brief moments at the beginning that my mother was just gone and in flight somewhere and she will return back to me.

Each time, this emotional experience has been triggered within the devastation of this loss. It has kept me in the unstable position on how I feel and my ability to trust the world and the people in it.

Inside I am this fragile little girl crying out for my mother, and each time I reach out for my needs to get reassurance, I found myself getting trapped inside those emotions as though that fateful day never seems to go away. This deep bond with my mother captivated my whole existence.

So the depth of grieving emotions is carried with me and those close to me always seem to know when I am not feeling my own balance and they come in to rescue me from my own emotional trauma of loss; inside there is a need to release it, but it took me a long time to grasp the idea of losing something of such a grand affair of love that I had with my mother.

To express or not to express

It's the unformulated fact we can't escape emotions and feelings as women. It's the little things that add up when others around you are expressing in full loads. You'd think humans would close tightly after the loss of a mother's love, but I have noticed people like to hold back on letting go, and I just wasn't ready to say goodbye to someone very special to me.

I had never known death to hurt as much as it does internally when the inability to express myself began getting me into unhealthy thinking, so I kept to myself. This made me realize trust was very vital with my mother and myself as a child growing up. I needed my mother to express to me on how much she loved me, and so in return, I shared this same expression with her.

I remember long ago I would love to buy flowers and a card for her on birthdays but even just out of the blue because I would feel her express to me in a lower tone and frequency, and it troubled my mind.

I noticed a few times coming from school, I saw this ache in her eyes, and so I would ask my friend to come pick me up and go buy some flowers and a card to perk her back up.

At the moment of surprise of the flowers, all the love would come flowing out of her again. This gave me reassurance that my love was enough for her, but the many times, I observed the frustrations in her eyes.

It began to hurt me, and I did not even notice because of learning suppression of my emotions, but I realized things were not going exactly as she had planned for some things in her life.

This made me grow a tougher mindset when I could feel that things were not right, but I could never figure them out exactly.

The sensations of being open or closed made a difference in my growth with being self-conscious of expressing myself or just holding it in. This made an impact on me when found that when I would express myself, everyone would make fun of me either at school or some friends that I knew growing up.

The best times were remembered, though, as I was very outgoing and loved doing things with my family; but then from time to time, I remember getting some ice cream at our favorite location. This kept me feeling like I was special within my family, but things inside of me turned ugly throughout my growth because the anger stage would do a number on my emotions and values in coping with a friend or even a loved one.

I would just break down and cry just out of nowhere, and then later my emotions began to explode, shattering everyone. I did not exactly like it at first because I would feel unbalanced afterward, then after a while, I just began to hold it in, then it made me begin to question whether to share my thoughts with anyone or keep it in. This was my hardest challenge of letting go and beginning the stage of liking me again when all hell would break open inside of me.

Something would trigger me, and there I go running away from the pain and feeling like no one understood me. I felt many times like everyone was abandoning me, but I did not know the loss was everlasting inside of me.

Dana's photography titled *Internal Tornado*

A CALL TOWARDS LOVE

Always falling inward into depressional states.

I had no idea I had shut myself down completely until lessons had to be seen and altered in those moments. The resentment would engulf me, and then I would explode, but what I was really wanting was not for this flame or spark back inside of me but to get back the feeling of love and to be loved.

Dana's artwork titled *Misunderstood Love>>*

This is an expression of seeing love but inside, not expressing it internally. It is standing all in it, but the passion and ignition switch is like turned off and no one can see it but me and everyone shows the direction inwards but the lack of seeing within the depression strangles the deep connection.

—Dana Gregory

This was a challenge in of itself: to begin the stage of acceptance about who I am and have become from the moment my mother decided her fate.

The devastation of having to face the emotions head on is everlasting of breaking all unsaid boundaries of the work of my mother and of myself of the grief.

I am a strong person, but this is the extreme, and I know God would not put me into a path that I could not handle. I sometimes think he made the wrong choice of my strength, and I know God knows more than me, but can I really do this on my own?

Then I realized that I needed to understand what I was missing inside of me and what I could do to change the outcome of the grief, and there was a door from a strange door knock, and I discovered something but at the time needed structure to handle things in my life.

My thoughts, emotions, and reactions began controlling the emptiness. It was chasing a rainbow that I would never see again in my life, and once you felt love from a mother like a rainbow, the endless need to replace it becomes the chase outwardly.

God's Love Attaching

But he was wounded for our transgressions, he was bruised for our iniquities, the chastisement of our peace was upon him, and with his stripes we are healed.

—Isaiah 53:5

A message comes straight to me as I hear a pull toward a strength never felt and a love of pureness, and he said, "I put you into it to grow and become stronger and you got what it takes to embrace this change inside of you for the love of me to you and this is the gift to your mother."

I cry out and say, "I am not the one for this," and he said, "Yes, you are, honey. I am here for you if you fall again, and I will send those to help you for that cry inside and for the deep ache of this loss. You can, my dear, rise above it, but you got to want too!"

I sat there crying even more because I did not understand what was going on within me. I cried for him to come back and me to go home with him.

The message reached out one more time and said, "You have all my strength—just reach for me and you'll see. I will pick you up and dust the cobwebs off and send loving people to guide your heart back into me and to the feelings and thoughts you need to bring about the change in which you came here to do for me." And I felt the presence left me.

I realized that maybe I was wrong in some of my thinking and behaviors, and so this depression began to give me more ache in my heart because I am here doing this work all by myself.

I am screaming in my pillow when no one was around. I am all alone and cold without my mother, and my aches began haunting me after the intensity of pain gushed through me.

I can't do this without my mother, and as I began to see other things engulf me, my tears just swelled up, and my eyes just gushed out more pain. I needed to be near my mother, and the deafening experience of my own emotions began sending more signals to my body.

I realized I was alone again, and the fear of abandonment crept inside of me. The sensations just melted into a pile of tenderness of love that hit me but only for brief moments. I vanished inside of me, and there I was standing within myself alone.

The dark clouds spiraled around me, and not knowing what to do or to handle this experience, I began to think my ego was acting according to the self, and the self was only seeing outside of me until I began seeing the obstacles in my way.

Dana's artwork titled *Alone>>*

Expressions of Grief

Ego is seeing the outside viewpoint of self vs.
seeing the inside of self and following the love.
When the ego is deflated within the shadow self
and groomed into nurturing the soul, balance
is corrected, and the self is bonded within.

The moments left me and I began to feel fear
and so I would escape and run or go call someone.

I would spend hours on the phone because this
gave the outlet of needing someone close to me, and
when the connection of feeling loss would come, I

would again feel the love and then loss. This began the stages of grief all over again.

It was like no escape from the deep loss, and the pain began to leave when I began to get close again with myself and with others.

Then I would get caught in denial of my own internal self. This began as a spinning wheel, and nothing would stop it until I closed my eyes, and then sleep would be the only thing that I could accept as a cleanser of the emotions and dried-up tears from something gone wrong in my life.

Mother and daughter's bond>>

3

I'd Rather Escape from
My Own Reality

The rush of expressing to others about love and related matters helped to decode my own inner struggle, and dealing with things on a more levelheaded way challenges me at certain times.

Grief and stress sometimes takes a lot of this emotional energy out of me, so I must sleep a lot when my body becomes low in energy or even when I get moody with my surroundings.

The circumstances undercoat the reality in which I make sense to others, but I get lost in the urge of really wanting to escape and not really cope with reality.

I think this is when stubbornness corners me into believing my outer world is much safer than my own internal world, and so I make choices which will give me that comfort of being safe and secure with my surroundings.

My bed has been a special friend when the outcomes are just too much to bare. I feel safe when I have no sudden jolts to my sensitive nature, and when I am sleeping, this gives me a sense of freedom without all the noise of the world around me. I think my balance comes back to me when the senses of my being become back in tune with my inner self and outer self.

One of the things that I have begun to recognize is the safety of being healthy and being me all in one place and being alone with myself. It has been taking a long time to appreciate this experience.

When I am home alone, fear overrides my expressions of being happy, and as I become more in sync with my life and my internal world, I find that I can achieve more things in my life.

The journey of really understanding stress and grief and the impact it creates in my own world has been a wondrous journey. It has been a roller-coaster ride knowing that I have been running through the fixation of grieving my mother's death my whole life. I discovered that it has been an unhealthy flow of the natural rhythm of my internal emotions.

This begins to help me understand how my own body works. I found that the fixation stage survivor mode has remained in a stuck position, and so when you clearly understand something and get some knowledge in how to change the circumstances, then one can begin the early flow back to being healthy again.

One other issue that I have read and discovered is that when the stage of being in grief stays on this fixation period, the bereaved phase of coexisting in my own reality also becomes fixated upon.

This phase has been running a long while since my mother had passed over forty years ago. I think when everything is going correctly, I find myself sliding back inside and forget all the importance of what has happened.

Life turns another corner, and there I am back again in the stuck position. I think I am going forward and the lessons return to me about my life and the function state just does not please me and my wants are not removed, or that is how it feels inside of me.

Then I feel like I am in the zone of not being in control of my own body, mind, and soul. There I am again stuck, unbalanced, and deep twisting moods spring out of me.

The experience makes me have the need for others to hear me, share my story over the phone or the problems that I face inside, but internally, I am scared to express the real stuff, so I share what is going on and I make things more fun by expressing jokes in nonfashionable way. This lightens my mood and I become less stressed and then I can move in another focused thought process and then I can begin to be a little freer inside.

I gently remove old thinking, and my emotions change, making my mood more positive. I just flip a switch, and there I go. I had forgotten what had happened from the moments before and the rest of the day is much more peaceful and my mood is happy the rest of the day.

Sometimes I just forget what the normal feeling is inside of me, and the natural flow of a healthy state of mind arises. I think this relates to recognizing my ability to listen and hear my voice say, "I am just angry at you" or "I am just sad about this in my life." I think this helps me to recall my inner self and how I really do feel about things. Then this stares right in front of me. I keep this hidden and then I forget and then I reflected upon my own internal expressions.

So I have noticed when my ego self is getting to esoteric, I must reel it back in and uncover my emotional states that is being out of balance, and I become fixated on my outer world and not on my internal world.

For example: I use to get into small arguments with someone, and I would project my emotions onto them. I liked it because I thought it felt good to release that anger that was going on inside of me at that moment, but then I had to rediscover that when I am using my emotions on the outside of me, I can no longer hear my internal world and what those emotions are inside of me.

My internal voice and dialogue softly says, "I am being squeezed out by this anger. Can you please stop it?" Then I close down my anger and begin to focus in the flow of good feelings, but underneath lies the depths of hidden anger. The flow still is following me, and I go with it anyway.

This is when I think I am going good and thinking and feeling rationally, but then when certain circumstances hit me square in the face, I am not dealing with my emotions on the inside of me, and I just reproject my emotions and thoughts onto situations.

I had no real clue that this was not normal, and so I wonder, did my mother have issues with this same particular problem?

Did my mother project the internal world outwards and then made the choice to end the frustrations and emotional conflict on the inside?

The devastations of losing and knowing that I have lost someone that I love internally makes me wonder about the emotional self that I carry. Is this the same love conflict that my mother had inside of herself before she decided to end it?

I know people pursue their own agendas for certain things, but I have never connected with other people and dealt with my mother's issues about committing suicide until now in my life.

I am thinking my mother had to have some internal issues regarding her ego and her inability to find emotional healing. I suspect that she was experiencing a deep agony pain of knowing that maybe my mother struggled with her own ego and the shadow self.

It is tough not understanding about your own ego states and how it relates to you and your own internal world around you. This gets me into thinking about denial and the many irrational states my mother had to go under of denying to partake in the actual experience and letting the emotions rule the inside and not being strong enough to withstand this mechanism of completing her journey here on earth with me.

Now my mind is going to wonder about this aspect of denial and how I must work through these phases of uncertainty so I do not make the same mistake of irrational thinking and begin cleaning my internal world.

Strangely, I am learning about the rational side of denial and the impact it creates within my own mind as a result of the devastating event of my mother's suicide.

Opening Love

Dana's photography titled *Cleansing Your Soul*>>

Receive the flow directly to you.

♡

I realized that yes, denial is real and one of the grieving stages, but when you think you have the clear functional or rational thinking about the word, it sits in front of you until the day comes when you have to deal with another issue landing in your lap.

You learn that it's just the beginning to completely understand that the mind can play tricks with you on a small scale and you get stuck in a pattern with no way out until someone points this out to you. This is an extreme wakeup call on the sensitive fixation side of normal feelings.

So one of the things that I discovered is that there is a conscious denial and unconscious denial, and boy, this has been a real awakening phase of the depths of understanding this on the real-world experience and not something you just read in a book.

This is about the mind of the child in a fantasy world and then coping with loss and the heaviest emotions within the self that can handle it in the moments autopilot kicks in.

Dana Gregory's photography titled *Hand in Nature*>>

The hands of God are pure of consciousness and make beauty with the creations that grants us onto this earth, but when the consciousness lives in the law of denial, the hand is on the outside of the law of harmony. This also speaks directly to your thoughts, words, and even actions when given the love.

The conscious denial is intentionally distorting the truth and making a story up. For example: a child leaves one cookie in the bag and ate the rest and has the mother concerned.

She asks the child, "Did you eat all the cookies but you left one cookie?" and the child responds to his mother with a made-up story that there was only one cookie in the bag.

The mother knows that the child is in a protective mode and that the child is owning his or her guilt but covering it up by stating there wasn't anything wrong and "I did not eat anything."

Most mourners defend against their own truth and inside create the false deceptions of the story being twisted but actualized in behavior or even though patterns.

The child is outright lying but tends to the emotional security of "If I lie, then mother won't know that it was me eating the cookies in the bag." But this stage creates a potential problem, and if not corrected, the unconscious mind absorbs it like a sponge and forgets to distinguish between the real truth and the lie. This outcome is displaced on creating a fictional story of their own life, and the denial captures the heart and mind of the child, teen, or even the adult.

I have come to understand this stage of denial had a cruel factor in my daily life as storytelling when I was young and wanted to feel important, but really inside, I just felt denial and nobody wanted me. This made me bounce in and out of the denial of consciousness and unconsciousness of rational and irrational thinking throughout my life. It made me cringe when I was making false choices in my past, and then I would run from my own mistakes and begin to say to myself, "That isn't my fault," and then project or throw the outcome away from my own inner dialogue.

It takes a lot to look deep at the reactions of ourselves and then be responsible for them if we act out with the wrong words or actions at somebody. Denial is a hard game, but once I have discovered that you no longer have to be in the denial phase and one can move past it quickly.

I really do, but it's just acknowledging my own reaction toward other people. This has the incredible misdirection in my life.

The growth has many challenges that one must face, and understanding the reactive side is the one that needs to be curved inward and channeled in healthy ways.

Yes, it's tough to channel love shock it's us in a moment's notice, and the anger arises from other things; but if the soul is cleansed from the dark mass energy which is the channel of the anger, then if seen as the wholeness of anger does to the body and mind.

The mind would avoid at all cost of reacting in this energy field, but it is tough when learned responses are embedded into a comfort zone.

Getting your way with anger is not healthy and it is a separating energy anyway and God is not about being separate from things. Remember, he is in all things. It is unity that grows, not anger, but the wholeness of the inner child being spoiled thinks it needs its way and anger is the only way to see this and then acting out in aggression and never remembering love in that moment.

Mother and daughter's bond>>

4

The Battle of Rejection

Sadly, my grief has plagued me for long periods over the course of my life, and it has guided into self-acceptance and loving the inside of me; but when I get overwhelmed for long periods, then I begin to unravel the circumstances of this battle again.

This battle of my ego and seeing things on the outside of me and not looking deep inside and seeing my own flaws still continues. This creates havoc inside of me again, so the battle continues but with a little more rational thinking and behaving.

Stress comes knocking at my door when I get overwhelmed with all my emotions and thinking in what all I have to accomplish in a day's time, so the battle of rationalizing out my day and my emotions comes at the forefront when I am seeing a new day, and some days, the bed looks more pleasing to the eye than chores or tasks in front of me.

And now, O Father, glorify thou me with thine own self with the glory which I had with thee before world was. (John 17:5)

This book of the law shall not depart out of thy mouth: but thou shalt meditate therein day and night, that thou mayest observe to do according to all that is written therein: for then thou shalt make thy way prosperous, and then thou shalt have good success. (Joshua 1:8)

I know everyone loves to snuggle with their blankets and enjoy the warmth if it is cold outside, but stress begins when I realize the days seem like they run in the same pattern and then I climb out of bed, thinking and feeling, *Is this a normal day of*

feeling, or is this an uphill battle with my depression/ grief? And then as my mind races inward on my sub-consciousness, I think, *Oh, boy, is this the day that I am going to be in a good mood or not?*

Most days, I am wanting to have a clear and functioning day, and then all of a sudden, another trigger hits me out of the blue, and there I am stuck in a pattern of thinking and dealing with my ego running the shots.

My ego is only seeing the outside of other people's emotions, and then I absorb this and think is it a rational behavior, and then I get into trouble later in the reactive response of my thinking and feeling toward things.

Then I climb back into my rut of stubbornness and irrational thinking, and the battle begins with having to deflate this ego state. Outside thinking patterns become an outrage outcome, but then I began to recognize my thinking and feeling in those moments.

So there I am, crushed internally with my sensitive self. There I am again facing the five grieving stages within me—denial, anger, bargaining, depression, and acceptance. The battle continues as each stage takes its course with me.

Dangling all the pieces around internally and wondering if the cycle will ever stop and regain normalcy, but the battle of the acceptance of change from the inside of me arranges itself, and then I seem to get lost within my own deceptions and illusions of thinking and feeling like I am a child standing in front of my parents and getting accused.

I discover new information from reading and listening to others because I am open to recognizing that something is wrong with this pattern, but then I come to the battle again and see I just can't accept the fact that my mother is gone and not with me.

The tug of the war begins again, and irrational thinking reemerges. I loved my mother, and everything we did together was everlasting to me. The pause seems real to me, and the focus of those emotions are the crying spells I can't seem to unravel. After each crying spell, I get up and feel better and then begin bargaining with myself.

"Well, this was only temporary today," and so I go and look for food and then I get comfort and then go on with my day as nothing had happened, but what I forgot to think about was recognizing that I was going into the acceptance phase of my mother being gone for so long.

So I have come to terms that I have to address my thinking and my emotional outbursts with a proactive approach. The rational and irrational mind play tug of war with me, and so does my ego and inside of my shadow ego. I have learned through trial and error that the proactive approach to this short-term gain is understanding the acceptance phase.

This will help to break away from bondage of distrust with myself and learning to forgive myself and others in a verbal manner. I must consider other people's values and learn what are healthy values regarding the level of trust and love that I have for myself.

The layers that form around acceptance is held together with love and also includes trust, respect, and honesty. The journey inward about accepting means that I may be concerned with my own rational mind of my mother's love.

This is going to be hard to accept because my love is so deep and I bonded with her that I dare believe my mother was really struggling with her emotional states.

My mother was my internal glue that held things together, and the chaos would occur when I was younger. My mother looked like she had it all together, and when I needed her, she was there, giving me a smile; and so when I reflect back on my memories of her, I can realize we did have some issues like all families do when a crisis occurs around the holidays.

I do recall a few times that there was a sense of a gloom in her eyes and there was a lot of disappointment going on and so I think there had to be some kind of issues that she must have held internally like I do around other people. I do think a lot of people do this but just do not share it.

Silently, I think to myself, *Does this happen in all families, or was this just mine because I had a different experience with my mother and my life?*

Then I question internally, *Was there enough help back then in the 1970s?* I am not really sure about that from a point of view of psychology, or maybe it was just slowly coming out that people were having issues and there was not enough support for them in those days.

I think my mother would have jumped at the opportunity to seek out psychological support and healing; and if she did, maybe over time, the issues coming to the surface would be addressed because things began to be more open in the eighties and nineties.

Now in the early twentieth centuries, we are in the day and age of information at our fingertips, and finding solutions to problems is much easier and faster with the Internet and the fast pace of things now. However, there are different methods in learning through reading books and discovering within social engagements.

The experience of being within the social functions with other people—this will give the feelings of support and safety with your environment.

This helped to engage in myself on how well I was adapting from the loss/grief internally and learning through communicating with my grandmother, friends, and my father. There was a certain time back then after my mother passed away I became numb and began isolating my own raw emotions, and so this took on a different turn when I began escaping the pain until I reached an understanding the pain which was keeping me locked in and couldn't move within my own emotional state . So I discovered that I wasn't alone and that they had grief groups and I joined with them and then I discovered that grief has many other levels to it—the mourning stages and proactive approaches to heal from grief and even my stages of stress, which are the four tasks of mourning.

Dana's photography titled *Firm Support*>>

The journey of weakness needs a strong foundation
that it can lean on through the troubled roads ahead.

—Dana Gregory

The adjustment phases within these four active approaches will have to come gradually as I recognize the value in which they hold for me and how I can use them wisely and with good intent for my further growth and achievements in my own life.

Standing within the grips of holding on to my mother's love is opening the wounds back up, and this is a frightening stage for me. This means that I have to realize the memories that I can't remember of my mother or my past has to surface and then feel the pain in a rapid stage and release it for my internal growth of letting go.

This will be own internal challenge that I must face regarding loving my mother and letting go of the love I have for her and then finding my identity in this mix.

This means internally, I have let go of the memories in which I do not recall a lot of them, so this will be challenge in front of me. I need to understand the rational and irrational thinking and emotions inside of me and separating the two of them.

Where do I belong, and where does my mother belong in this scenario of love?

This begins to boggle my mind, and doing this on my own is going to be rough in terms of understanding the mixture of emotions of my mother and me regarding love.

First thing is understanding how love is supposed to feel in a healthy obstruction with families and the dynamic of a functional system about love and loving inwardly and externally since I have been in numbness for a long time now. I think this is where my own boundaries and even understanding has been mis dialed within my storage of rational thinking and feeling.

I have to come to terms with the basis of who I am and who I want to become inside of me, and then I can begin to see the difference of my own identity and my mother's identity.

Where does this strange feeling come from inside of me? And what does it all really mean when you say, "My own identity"? The inner infant may be afraid in regarding the trust level it has for the adult self.

This is the phase of separating the internal voices and impressions and even memories and even emotions. This is when the work can begin on the next phase, which is understanding of the different aspects about my own knowledge about love and the acknowledgment of what is real love, so I do not accept another false pretense about love and loving my own soul and body.

The challenges unravel inside of me, and the questions begin rapidly compiling in the argumental phase with myself and a friend.

Is there really a defining line about love? And who's to say, "My love is not healthy," and so a friend may ask you, "Are you really happy internally?"

If this questions or subline comes into play of "No, I am not really happy," I think some things could change and be a little better with my life. Then the phase of questions is going in the internal link with yourself and how you really feel on the inside.

Can I be happy when my infant self is the one crying for something else? Another question may arise, and that is "Am I too numb or in denial to feel my own infant self?"

So this is where the mind has to begin to go in and analyze what the words are being presented on the internal dialogue computer screen within your brain signals of what you are consciously and unconsciously thinking within listening to your own thoughts or even words that were expressed outwardly to others.

Then you have to ask yourself, does this match the reality of the goals for yourself and the internal reward system of love? If you are on the level of five on an emotional feeling list, then you're not always feeling the ten like most people feel on a regular family system.

Then you must go internally and find the answer that keeps you stranded or stuck in a phase you really do not accept on a regular basis for yourself.

The first question to ask yourself is do you love your inner child? And if so, how does this feeling come across from the inside of you? Is there a low residue of blackness surrounding the child within or numbness in those feelings? If the answer is yes, then you must do the inside work to recover those lost emotions as a child.

This comes in as an investigator part but not as the authority figure wanting to rip apart the infant self. The infant self is probably not trusting of the adult self, so this has to be handled with caution and with sensitivity or even curiosity.

Questions may come in as to the whys of the importance of this work, and the answers will be conveyed back to you. This is the bond in which you began to form the stages of love and the bond you had with your mother inside of the womb and the growing phases of love with your mother.

When you can come to acceptance that this work is the importance of the acceptance phase, then your life can be healed as long as you are willing and able to accomplish this goal for yourself and for others around you.

When you make this hard and enduring commitment internally to heal whatever has been lost or even broken with this bond, this is when healing can truly begin at the stage of acceptance of grief or the loss of a mother.

This is when the reality of growth must grow into being honest and seeing the reality as it is in front of you and not what you accept as the real truth inside of you. This is when the challenge of respect for yourself and trust will be present itself inside of you, when you begin to open to door for love for the infant self.

The nest phase is on the level of being honest and lying with your dialogue with yourself and with your infant self. If there is a moment, internally, of a foggy emotional experience, then this fog is a made-up story from the inner child's dialogue on how she was experiencing either in the womb or on the outside of the world. You have to get the inner child to trust you again then ask questions when she shares this information to you.

Now if there is a sign of stubbornness coming, then this is a sign from either your teenager side or the infant self trying to protect itself. This is the challenge of the circumstances of helping the crying infant self and the adult within.

There are many questions that must be asked in order for the child to be honest and trusting the adult self. This is where the parenting aspect comes into play. If the parents were strict, then the following mode may be a stretch to climb but if there was some room to play, then this is the area in which you can open the communication of the soul and the growth within.

If you can rise with it and become open and allow this process to come about, then love will eventually be awakened by your infant self, but this is your challenge if you want it.

Mother and daughter's bond

5

The Reality and Responses about Honesty

The value of helping the infant self is the growth and maturity that comes with being open to the reality and the emotional states of the growth inside with the stability at hand.

The infant self wants to feel that you are being honest and loving toward growth and even maturing but as humans we get into goal-oriented approaches to handle things, and this is a good sign for the adult self because you are allowing the trust to open and the honesty comes with the delicate approaches of love from the adult self.

Going internally for growth

Now for the infant stage, there is more of an energy level of understanding on the emotional wavelength. They understand in terms on how you feel internally rather than goal-oriented facts about things.

In the early development as an infant, if you remember as an infant yourself or if by watching an infant react to the world, if you cannot recall those memories, then you are in the liquid phase, after coming out of the liquid womb of the mother. The infant self is still coming out of this stage. The sounds and lights are very scary because it is in the unknown phases of acknowledging the situation the soul, spirit has come into a new body.

The frightening phase is the depths of understanding when the baby is beginning the emotional acceptance on where it is and what is going to happen around itself. This is the beginning stages with having abandonment emotional experience, and so, if the mother was not around the infant at certain times and the comfort level began to be stressful, then the infant self only knows fear and then becomes angry and cries for the attention.

You can recognize this phase with yourself when you do not get your way. How or what is the emotional response from this outcome? This is the beginning stages of awareness as an infant self. This is the stage in which the adult self must go through in order to understand the maturity levels of what has not been learned, or you have to relearn because of the dysfunctional governing of parental guides of their information, but parenting can play in the situation as well.

So if the infant self grows up in a dysfunctional setup and is afraid and angry, then when it comes to siblings, there may be a rival game present with the inner growth of this infant self. This takes us to the personality growing with a passive-aggressive nature which inherits an infliction with aggressive behavior. This is due to the inner child not always getting his/her way or the physical desire being met as the infant, and resentments occur a little faster with the ego inflated, and the dark shadow has created an imbalance within the child self as the infant self.

Jealous people and brain connection

A particular monkey's brain can only see the results of interaction as a threat and, thus, react in a manner other than normal, which is hasty attitude toward other humans or even animals.

This depends on the level of maturity and how well the adaption phase works with the infant self and the inner adult self. This has many directions it can lead to, but the main lead is the interaction and feeling a threat internally as the reaction outwardly occurs with situations. This results in a fierce jealousy within their character, and when things do not suit them, they will look for a deepening fault and destroy the beauty for what suits them in the moment.

These people are feeling threats around them and project this on others within their jealousy. The threat feeling can exhibit a sense of loss but could be labeled internally wrong or locked in the denial phase, and so the acceptance of this behavior goes directly into reaction mode, and one sees the results but fail to recognize there is a consequence to this reaction.

The monkey brain can only see the shadow of ego at work, and so this infant self of the human has grown to hate and not internally love things, or they can't honestly see beauty as it once was before the infliction of pain of loss.

This pain has been engaged in a short-tempered rage on the self for whatever reason, rather self-induced, with own deceptions of infant self which has turned against itself and the beauty within, or this could also be linked to other abuse forms in childhood or later in life. It all depends on the functional state of receiving the messages.

Infant self can no longer see beauty in life and so the monkey brain takes every situation as a threat, but underneath is the fear of being understood and recognized as a beautiful monkey with clever ways of approaching life.

This can be reduced in lower doses, but the reaction mode has to become aware of the words being expressed outwardly: which is taking the openness, awareness, receptors in listening and recalling, non-judgmental reactions to self and self-acceptance with another approach to the expression of words spoken outwardly to others.

The monkey brain has to reconcile the inner conflict and discover love again. This is the responsibility of the adult and coming to terms with self-managing the infant or child inner conflict. This is also the phase of understanding learning to respect and trust the internal world of the infant self.

Infant maturity with abandonment

The mother's gifts of love to an infant is to give emotional support, comfort, security, and safety, and this is the responsibility of a mother to the infant as it grows and matures through the early phases of development as the beginning stages occur.

This is the fundamental value which holds the structure of giving and receiving the gift from a mother to the infant about love in regarding the natural rhythm of nature. This is a critical focus direction within the mother and the infant bond. This is the stage in which the healthy love can grow and mature throughout its lifespan.

Now when the mother cuddles and coos the infant in a special way, the bond may begin to express uneasiness within the infant's security and safety because then the infant absorbs this information and reacts in a fundamental way with crying.

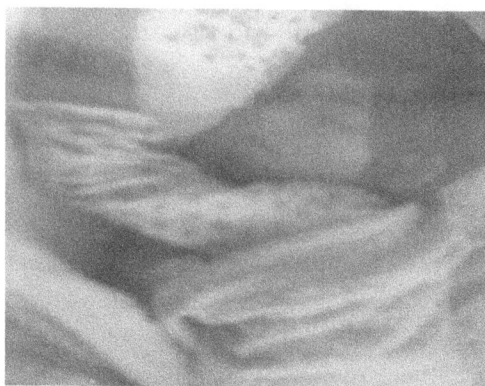

Lori

*The Flower bud still sleeps, when shall the bud
bloom in the wakening of the morning.*

—Dana Gregory

The infant self registers the surroundings and
equates the information and allows it in but becomes
confused if the mother is giving an off signal that she
is in an emotional and dangerous territory of inade-
quacy within her own emotional expressions about
love with regarding an unhealthy living space.

Then the infant is obscured into believing
the fundamental values of observing, reacting, and
trusting the security of the environment as does the
mother in those moments, so the environment is
expressing unorganized thinking and feeling toward
the infant.

The infant is learning and is very receptive to
an unhealthy emotional attachment in being disor-

ganized internally, and so this begins the stages of growth through the mother's conviction of bonding with love but conveys a small signal of trust within the bonding.

This is the average sign of disorganized emotional expression about love, honesty, and the reality it is forming unless the mother can correct this through her devotion of love through the infant to the child growing up.

The surrender of the love is the part that can get complicated with the infant self and child growing up if the mother has functional boundary system from the internal point of view. This will help build the quality of the character within the infant self.

Now if there was blurred boundaries being conveyed in the cross-connection with the child then later in the child's life, the teen and adult self will carry these levels from the mother's internal process of information. This is not necessarily a bad thing regarding the forward motion of learning and breaking the dysfunctional system of parenting apart.

Where there becomes a crisis is if the child is bearing this internal work and not corrected, then life gets in the way of the early stages of understanding the emotional infant self. This can carry on into other stages of growth and boundaries about emotional behavior when a loss occurs in a family.

So later in life, the surrender process leads into the vital stage of understanding through the emotions of the infant, teen, and adult in exploring the child behavior even as the adult. These stages carry with us from birth and is our baggage which we hold onto in the near future of the adult self.

Now where the deep concern becomes if the child learned how separate identities with healthy boundaries or did the child become too coddled and cooed through each stage of development, which the impression of an ideal princess or idol if-you-will mentality as the child growing up with the intentional dysfunctional behavior in the accordance of irrational disturbance in the emotional waves of energy carried through to the next stage.

Now the reality sets in for the stage of honesty within the infant, child, teenager, and the adult self. Am I normal in thinking and feeling, or is there an imbalance within my growth that may have hampered with my internal process of growth and I would not even had known it?

Emotionally feeling is a great thing, and we do this consciously or unconsciously, given a normal standard of being accepted in life. Again, now is another critical point to rationalize regarding the stability of one's own emotional expressions inwardly and outwardly toward others. This connects with the abundance levels of healthy and unhealthy behavior and the attachment levels within the infant, child, teen, and adult.

The questions remain inside as the observer (you) examines the outbursts of reactions, behaviors, cognitively expressing on the inside of the processor of the brain waves from the infant self to child self to teenager self and to the functional adult self.

Did your parents create a legacy of thinking and feeling toward things or the simple values you hold within your three characters? You or someone else can be the observer of the reactions and behaviors of what needs adjusted, but in the long run, the choice is left up to you.

Now here comes the comfort level that everyone loves to commit to on the inside of the self. This is interconnection with all those stages of growing up as the infant, child, teen, and then to the adult self. Now as the adult self, the other characters involved also hold onto this comfort stage.

Lori Weaver, age 12 years old>>

The delicate flower expresses and eludes over the semantic of love, and the wholeness is rendered with a gentle love.

—Dana Gregory

Which character is the main or dominate character that runs the road of this comfort?

Is this the character of your mother, or is this your character within your father's make-up?

Now we are getting into the abandonment of those stages of growth and losing self-identity.

The questions that must be asked within those characters: Did I lose my infant, child, teen self while growing up with my parents? And if so, who or what emotions are attached to it? Then the next question comes in: Is there an identity issue with me?

The next several stages involved become crucial in asking these questions to the self.

After the stages of losing someone that you loved, are there phases in between stages of behavior of emotions that occur outwardly that you can recognize with yourself?

Grief bares many stages of loss in the emotional selves in those characters. Are there fears, (aloneness—abandonment), anger (built-up frustrations that lead to resentment toward self or parents), guilt, separation of identity, and not being honest with self and/or self-expression (lies internally to self), remorse (actions or thoughts that created tension in self), numbness (closed-in, locked-up emotions, feeling caged in of no other routes of acceptance internally, and/or addiction to some form of chemicals [example: sugar, caffeine, street drugs, and/or alcohol]).

These all bear fruit with evolvement of those characters and their own self- identities. If there is a gap between memories or lost memories, then there is work there to improve those inner in balances of self.

Yes, self-exploring is the toughest road of finding out the real you, but if you make or accept this challenge or the choice therein, you do evolve as a whole person without feeling the abandonment or loss of emotions from the self, and you continue to grow; but if you choose the challenge inwardly, then what you are actually saying to yourself is that "I'm not good enough to evolve," then you have to live with the consequences of failing self and those parts of you.

Then the spiritual side of you fails God and the image of the creation that he created, so you are harming the birth right of evolving as a soul through, and then resentment creates the whole in which the soul can't return to unless the brain of the adult self wants to create "the law of harmony of God internally."

Then the soul will adapt to the change, and the resistance of being the soul of God will eventually change, but you want the road of "no self-identity," then you're adapting to the road of the diverse actions against intentions for you.

This is false self (fake) identity which creates disharmony with nature and then causes the intense water ripple effect around your environment. These delusions of creating the narrative of "I need someone else to do this work for me," then what did you learn from God and thy self in the self-acceptance of the real soul of God?

It's like you're telling God that you are not worthy of his love, and so "I am not worthy of self." Then suicidal mind takes over and then the belief systems and actions stepped forward unless the brain changes the course of thoughts. The end result that occurs can be death.

A mother's love and devotional expression of suicide to their own infant, child, teenager, and then to the adult carries these messages to their own child which she created. This is an enduring long and hard balance of knowing boundaries within self and knowing these are the stages in which the mother that did commit suicide carried that forward to the infant and child that she created in God.

Then the child is left with those emotions expressed until the adult self can withstand the storm and drive into the challenge and break this internal expression of the self, then love and harmony will be restored and rectified through the love of God.

The lessons of a mother and daughter's love connection can and does rebuild, but it is up to the child to either carry this forward in the legacy or change it for further growth of love to transpire through the future of love.

Mother and daughter's bond

Delicate memories of connection and the sense of pride of have loved a genuine soul, like my mother.

—Dana Gregory

Mother and daughter's bond

6

Learning to Be Open

The expression of love heals the departed when the devotion surrenders to the grace of harmony and the foundations are restored from the inside out.

—Dana Gregory

Grieving takes on a different layer of stress with the emotional self, and the physical signs become evidence.

The soul feels under attack even when there is a trigger presented inside of the lost feeling even after thirty or forty years had passed from a loved one passing. This can cause disharmony with the nature of the internal self.

This same feeling of a trigger can spring on, and it does not have to be related to any loss, but it could be a friend becoming ill to a loss of an animal but returns back home to the internal self. This too can trigger the solid foundation within the feeling of loss if the loss or grief has not been properly dealt with from the inside out. The trigger is for you to recognize the signs of stress internally but mainly for the alarm phase. This is a good sign for the body to prepare itself.

Infants are born with no recognition of death, and so for the infant self to acknowledge the signs of death, there is no language because all they know inside that their inner self is an awkward experience in emotions with the parents or caretakers.

The infant can register the emotions of tears and internally receive and process information in their own processing minds. They can create an outgoing experience of their grief. This affects the inner knowledge of the truth about living as a child in the world.

This makes the infant begin to question self when faced with a death especially if this was one of the first experiences of a loss. The infant can't relate to this information, only that there is love and unity, and negative energies enter anything that there is something being divided at a higher scale.

In return, the infant calls to the adult self to explain the truth of what happened and why there is pain going in and around the souls. This is why the infant cries and then gets comfort from the parent or caretaker. If this is an adult dealing with grief, then all children will discuss within the adult self to make clear sense of the experience.

Now when certain parts of the adult self, like the infant, child, and teen, cannot speak, this means there is a block of energy that just needs to be purged out, and then the proper care for the adult self can release. Then the body can correspond to the loss and then process it out.

There are some exceptions to every situation when dealing with death and the final areas of the end cycle. Suicide is a cycle all on its own language, but for the most part severe punishment hits the family hard because this is an act done with intentions.

For an infant or even as a child or teenager, there are many questions that run through the mind as the funeral is going on or even way after the experience is long gone. The question may plague the individual for a long time.

The general aspects of the inside consciousness energy waves within connects only with thinking about life, and the unconsciousness may reject this with degrees of denial because this is easier than coping with a life with the parent that committed suicide.

The deep question arises about the quality of the inner self and may have a dialogue with the infant, child, or even the teenager within. If my parent can just up and leave with no hesitation of unity and love, then there is something wrong with me from the infant and child self.

The moral of this dialogue is that I am not worthy of love and to be loved from an infant or child perspective because remember, the infant self only knows life and unity within love.

When the notes of the singing soul reside in a happy tone, the infant knows the heavenly feeling and love from God and the unity that he created in the essence for our souls to evolve and create more harmony toward a life of love.

The suicide upsets one's core values and beliefs because it is a selfish act toward the soul. It crushes the infant's soul because the infant only wanted to feel loved and supported. When the apple is split in two, so is the infant's soul when experiencing the love feeling. So the unity feeling is split in half, and the emotional self is also confused with this half circle of life and then the infant becomes strangled into a cycle it did not want internally.

The child begins to understand that he/she has a voice, which reacts in what it only knows is the split of the parent of love. This internal engrossed stitching has evolved into anger, and then the child can no longer accept love from the inside of the soul.

It is a battle of crying and not being accepted by someone, and so the child begins to unwind the ties of the split; and when the soul recognizes that there is a big difference after time has passed and the infant soul knows that there is love from a spouse or elsewhere, then it may overcome and rise to the challenge; but if the child is stuck in the midst of the storm of the split, then the love pattern inside of the relationships will follow along the same pattern created with the parent and suicide-focused directions.

Sometimes this is not what is wanted but is formed within the nontension avenue, and with this is a high resolution of highly intense tensions that begin to create more routes of frustrations inside of the marriage later in life especially when the grief inside has never been truly dealt with for the long term. We often do not have time to deal with grief and the loss of emotions, so this always goes on the back burner; and then when tensions are built within the relationship, it directly comes into play with the two of them.

If they chose to deal with the grief, then life can begin the cycle of repairing itself; but the stage of denial is prevalent, then it is in the obvious signs within the relationship itself.

These generally are small arguments, and then there are even harder times when loss knocks at the door and the adult self says, "I do not have time to deal with this emotional stuff right now." Later in life, it will become the center in which the health declines and the mind can no longer take on the stress and then the body begins to slowly decline.

The average person can only come into grips with a certain level of pressure, and the cracks appear when life gets in the way. It's a normal experience, but when the emotions are not healed again, there is a storyline of blockages inside of the chakras, and the organs begin to follow along the signals being sent to the body.

You see, when anger is stored, it affects the liver, and guilt is stored in the kidneys. The fear gets stored in your lungs, and there is another focus to be concerned with—is the resentment, envy, jealousy, greed, which are stored in the colon. So if there are health issues, then the body has not properly dealt with those hidden secrets stored in memories in the body.

The body is the one that shares the hidden secrets even when the mind won't acknowledge the pain. The body will be honest with the emotional healing that needs to be dealt with and gives you the signals to alarm you that you have a problem internally that needs to be dealt with on the inside of the mind so that the body can flow back in balance as the infant self.

Death, stress, and health issues are all linked with one another, and so when you are dealing with trauma or blocked emotions in the chakra centers, then it will open up the healing to begin; and if you deny them, the body will scream until it gets what it wants to fix itself.

Family dynamics

Every family carries different stress roles in the dynamics within the trauma or death of a loved one. Now is the time to recognize what style you used back when the loss occurred with death. This could be an early death of a life of a child or teenager and even a young adult—a suicide, car accident, murder, and/or illness.

These roles that are played are fairly obvious, and other roles may not be as obvious. Dad may have been the authority figure, the mother the caregiver, and the aunt historian, a cousin a martyr, and someone always shows up as the star of the show. During a loss of a loved one and the funeral time, the characters internally seem to react in accordance to the play of the real character. However, the stages of these roles pop out when the beginning stages occur with mourning.

Characters: the authoritarian steps up and plays the main dominate leader as the producer-director and taking care of all funeral arrangements. The caretaker is the one who makes sure all of the needs are being met, and the martyr complains he has been wronged in some way.

Now opening the love channels and understanding you played a part play out of the scene and that how you reacted is normal, but it matters if this still affects you in some small way in life now. Are you still playing these characters and you may not even realize it? Can you remember who played what as the character in a movie screen within the memories?

Family members>>

Strength built around the solid foundation of love and the enduring experience is priceless of understanding wisdom through someone else's eyes.

—Dana Gregory

Relationships are formed around attachment and detachment. This is also including friends, family, lovers, and spouses.

Family

Neutral

Attachment

Detachment

Friends

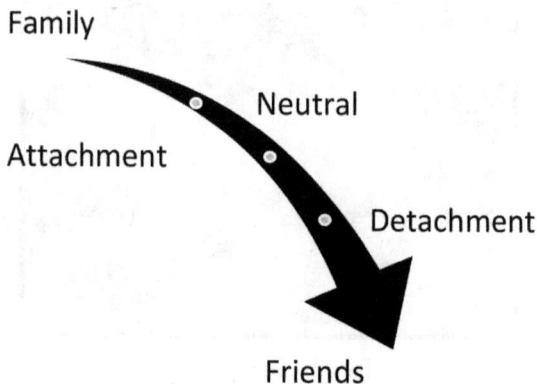

The neutral stance shows a normal behavior in balance when it comes to attachment or detachment to material objects, people, places, and even with spiritual beliefs.

Now remember, roles can be inverted in other ways in our lives—maybe another death and you're in a different position and on another family angle of focused thoughts or in less devotion to things or maybe still stuck in motions of grief.

There are those certain times in family dynamics that the authority-director and producer may be so engrossed in the control mode that it slips out and then tries to control every scene and this focus mindset, including the way someone should grieve and/or allow someone to feel their own grief because the desire of the controller needs to feel that things are set in motion.

The caretaker is so obsessed about other people's needs that it tends to be an object to reject her own emotions in the process and then later in life. They can take other roles of the authority- director of the household, and it also plays with the other characters—the emptiness of the martyr of "everything happens to me" attitude and then the star in the crowd.

Roles can exchange with characters, or they all can be absorbed into the whole system of the family dynamic in which everyone plays these certain characters all the time in a different sequence of layers within the lines. So now, by examining your awareness and how you played in these parts when the death occurred, then at least you are at the beginning stages of opening the channels so the healing can be understood and why certain outcomes play out when no one is paying full attention and understanding the methods of the inner worlds of the family.

Each person carrying these roles must heal those wounds inside, or otherwise, the effects turn into a deeper dysfunctional system, then you are dealt with more aggression on different layers. This could be played as passive-aggressive and then aggressive, but then the victim comes in and then they need rescued.

These are vital in role playing with family members. Everyone hurts when someone dies, but it does not need to be extended through abuse through aggression because the lack of understanding what they see on the outside is not always the case of what is going in on the inside of the person.

Jealousy, envy, and even greed can pass through the different roles with the dysfunctional system, and the game is not balanced in the family. Then the role of the authority has to play the controller until things become balanced.

The proper structure in a family is the sense of balance, security, and self-worth; but when the dysfunctions are centered and the control goes back to the people in which they need to take the balance off the authority-director so that the balance of roles of each character is building, holding, protecting their own responsibilities, then life can begin to surface to wholeness.

It's tough to face or deal with a big family dynamic, and when the authority figure takes over, all he or she wants is the balance to circle fast so he can find the balance within him/herself.

When the caretaker comes into play, then all they want internally is get on with being responsible of their own emotions, which is grieving the loss and not having to be in the direct spotlight of meeting other people's needs. This can be focused energy and then as a codependent to the authority figure, but this is when they need to step in and be independent in the big dynamic characters.

Life can be a struggle to find the balance, but when it is found and the load is taken off, the soul can cleanse through healing the inside

A CALL TOWARDS LOVE

Tractor of love from the family line

*Expressing the curiosity of a teenager and knowing
my family is near for me, the lessons learned of the
inner struggles of balancing the soul within love.*

—Dana Gregory

The martyr is the fragile one who is internally very sensitive. They take things to heart and are crushed when not successful. They beat themselves down as well as their own credibility within the belief system.

Everyone is out to get them, and then the characters of the family begin to avoid the sensitive one because the victim can't seem to find their own role or identity in the mix, and so they value emotions, but this can lead to the negative aspects which the emotional self can't control things on the physical level because they are processing the grief in another way.

This can affect the dynamic in a negative functional system when the martyr is out of control of their own emotions and can't let go of the emotional grief. They may tend to take this out in other formats on the family dynamic system.

Then life becomes a major dysfunctional system and out of sync of healing, and then scars of the anger have not begun to heal in order for the grief to pass. If this martyr is in a constant state of imbalance, disorganized, and not in control of his/her emotional state, then the patterns of it all play in a circle format.

The structure for the martyr has been set up for the emotional scars to heal without control and then lifted by balance. He/she has to find balance inside of her inner conflict and in the self-worth, self-discovery, and self-identity process. They are processors of the emotions of the system.

If this system can't find balance and the martyr is playing all those characters of everyone else, then he/she is the one which needs to do the most work inside of grieving, but this is also dynamic if the inner infant has not had self-identity, then it becomes harder for the growth to mature as fast as the other characters in the family dynamic.

Finding self-worth and self-identity

The first thing in grief healing everyone must understand is the fundamental aspects the person feels toward their own self. This doesn't mean just the physical self. There is more in this focus direction.

Finding self-worth is knowing that you are a soul of God, and in this you will see unity.

Early teenager foundation>>

Accelerating and Achieving through the bumps and roadblocks in front of me and climbing above the rest as I was wounded by the sense of loss of mother .

—Dana Gregory

Only then can you see a sense of self- worth because the creator created you in his image. So God is the light and love of this circle of self-worth and even in self-identity and unity. When you find internal unity and feeling of being inside of a unit, then the process of feeling alone inside will vanish.

Separating from people is a good thing as long as you are still separating yourselves internally, which could mean that if there is a disconnect within the infant self within the self-worth, then there is a deep issue to resolve; and if the inner child or teenager is dealing with self-identity, then there is work there as well, so the focus of the emotional healing is to dig at the roots of loss and remove it.

This means the martyr needs to take in the road which she is running from when feelings of isolation and loneliness take over. The loneliness is the center command center or the star, authority figure which is not taking on the grief in a responsible way to heal and grieve the mass index of emotions that are stored internally, and so the pain remains inside.

Until they reach the bliss healing factor inside of them, it will be stuck or blocked internally with them. This is the stronghold of depressional states in which the mind/memories are fragile to the infant self and inner child, but this is when toughness has to come out.

They have to take it on as a deep commitment to dig at the guts of it and remove the icky or hurtful feeling, and the mindset should be focusing on the exercise that you have to feel it to heal it.

Grandmother and Lori

When enduring heaviness of a rock that fell on you by accident. It takes a team to rebuild the foundation and with the extreme levels of confidence so it provides a knowledge of love in return.

Mother and daughter's bond

7

Standing Side by Side

*To know thyself is to love thyself and to be in
center with unity, in sync with universal laws
and with all authentic characters of self.*

—Dana Gregory

The direction of thinking with low self-worth
and self-identity issues can open unwanted doors in
the unknown spiritual portals in which the shadow/
ego self can dictate the process of centering with this
world than the authentic self.

When the authentic self is separated from the
infant, child, teenager, and/or all inside of the adult
self, this can call on unwanted spirits to enter into
you. The soul is not mature enough and lacks the
tools in which to fight off those entities that want to
attach themselves to you.

You see, if the spiritual world has a split system which can create an outcome for disturbance in the universe, then it can travel into other dimensions and/or portals. Earth has many portals and dimensions layered in from the scientific point of view.

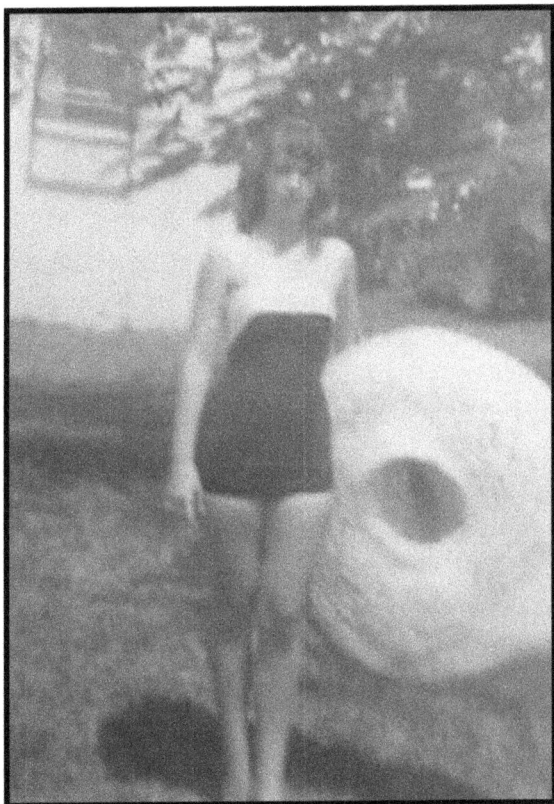

Lori's outdoor curiosity>>

*Knowing the edge of experiencing fun with
the absolute honesty within myself.*

—Dana Gregory

Now when we begin to talk about the spiritual side of things, we must talk about the law of duality, which means the opposition or contrast between two concepts of something. So now, we have the system within the spiritual side which is called the astral being. The astral side can travel within the dimensions, and this happens when we cross over after death. We are no longer a physical person in a physical world. We are now living in a dual reality in which the soul can move about in the space-time continuum.

There is a catch though. If you are not centered in the evidence of the soul and the soul parts of your spirit identity, then there is a major challenge when crossing over. Parts of you are going to be stuck within this dual reality, and other parts are split elsewhere until the karma has worked itself out or you have done the internal work to center the soul to travel inward bound inside of the universe through the dimensions.

Many individuals have a struggle with reincarnation, but scientists are now trying to prove that there is life after death; and what they have found is that if the soul has unfinished business here from a karmic point of view, the soul travels back to the earth channel and then be recognized and then be given a path to take in a forward direction.

It still is being proved, but they have to first understand the dimensions and then be able to discuss all the workings of it. There are many universities researching the death cycle and the process in which they survive in the afterlife. So by understanding, there is hope on the other side and even here on earth that we as humans are centering and evolving into a higher consciousness and creator from God.

However, we are in the here and now on earth and doing a lot of self-discovery about how the mind, body, and soul interact here on earth. If the characters (infant, child, teenager) are abundantly separated from one another, then the outcomes of depressions and the emotional self is feeling stuck or even locked in a sense of being alone because it is standing alone on the inside of self.

The counterparts of the whole self are considering to be forgotten in this world. The design of the creator's source intentions was to be centered within him, and thus, you are the God of his own image.

Most of the time, we center our focus on what we can control on the outside, but it is the inside that matters to God. He knows you will be successful when all parts are as one as like he is everywhere. This leads us with the intent in going inward to heal those characters and bring them back inside of the adult self.

The selfless actions of upturning the basket of healing is gaining the access in the real true character of the divine soul, but this means all of you must become centered in order to understand the climate of what God has to offer you. For example, when the mind and body do not flow correctly, the uphill challenge begins, and then you make mistakes because you are not truly centered in self. The real self is contained in a box and, thus, is blocked to experience the internal growth.

The battle of the ego is the main seat to focus on. When the ego is not flattened of the obsessions within those values, then of course, the irrational dysfunctional thinking is rationalized as normal thinking. This system creates a storm within a storm because this is way of the ego, and the darn ego rules over everything in sight.

The depth of healing and cleansing each part (characters) of the ego is knowing what is sitting in front of you. The depression sits on resentment which, in return, leads to fear and then coincides with being alone, and now when you examine the frame of mind of these stages, you will begin to see patterns.

These patterns are trying to tell you that "I am feeling alone because parts of me are missing, and therefore, I am devastated as a victim or martyr," the one who claims the sensitive side and also rules over the ego. This ego runs a lot of thinking patterns as well as the endless dysfunctional way of behaving.

The channel inward is going in with a downstream focus and revitalizing the emotions, and using the proper tools with diagnosing what the depths of the depressional state of mind is relying on the reward system and/or the negative outcome, which is losing something. Clinically, there is a psychological game we play as a human with our own selves. We usually play this mental mind game within our characters.

The infant self says, "My reward system for being in a negative wavelength is because I can let everyone else to do it for me, and so I will not have to work at all," but this is within the negative of loss, and so the mental ego is now going to play a game for the instructions on how to displace the interlocking patterns to play out in a sequences of events.

So the infant shares data from the processing center of the brain and sends out the signal to the reward and/or loss system, and then after receiving this picture from the infant to the child, then the mind of it begins to churn out that data from the beginning of the original thoughts being presented internally and outwardly through communication.

So now, when the brain waves receive this information and data that there is a stuck/blocked avenue, one signal it gives out is through the physical side and then out with the emotional side. These two signals go back and forth with one another until the body receives what to do with the data and then processes the information.

Now here comes a more complex and difficult problem that arises from this on the level of comfort. If the infant and child have been on the ongoing of the princess self, in which if "I play the sensitive child, then I can manipulate situations to get my way so I can have back my reward system," which is basically the infant/child's comfort zone, then nothing needs to change from the original thought processing.

It then goes deeper regarding the grief stages and loss system. If the child and teenager understood a rationalized comfort and uses resistance and/or stubbornness from any of these ages to gain access to the reward system, then you have a major and more complex system because the inner child has a comfort and the infant self has a comfort and now so does the teenager, but the adult self can rationalize out circumstances and knows when they see their grandchildren making irrational choices, but the depressional states are blocked with depression, resentment, and/or negative loss in the grieving system, then the adult self-churns out again resistance but also denial of the aches of pain that is being blocked.

Then an event occurs within the characters and outwardly acts out. Then the self-programing of reactions stands in play motion until the child's other characters run the course. This blockage contains vital information that needs to purge out from the place it is stored in so that way, the abundance of love can heal from God's energy levels. The acceptance of this challenge is wanting to downstream the pain and circulate the information the infant, child, and teenager have to say in order to balance within this cycle.

Acceptance of all working parts come in and share the inner wisdom learned from the back hold of those emotions and, in return, can and does replace the negative playback system as long as the process is in total working acceptance of the healing that will take place.

Now comes the hard parts of the inner circle of the characters and how to get to them and get them to want to help in guidance of balancing out the blocks. So now you will have to understand each character in which plays what role and the reactions it takes for the process to begin.

It is using the method of team playing and collectively giving them assignments to achieve, and this is how you can begin by saying to the child within, "Can you locate this memory and emotions and/or time and place in which it occurred?" and so forth within this work.

It will come—and maybe when you least expect it—because if the other characters are using the resistance code to block them, then this is where more work is required in the mix of wanting to combine all of you inside of the circle for balance and harmony to run it inside of you.

There will be at a certain time the inner child will want to run away and/or play games to manipulate the other characters to win and make the adult self lose for the program stays in stagnation rut and nothing can be altered until this range of emotions and thinking patterns are overturned internally.

This takes the authority-director side in making hard choices for the infant, child, and teenager selves. This takes hard commitment and dedication in resolving the inner maxed out system that had been plagued for years. You can master this by also using the iron control grip of the adult self for in the inner work of the other characters that are really desperately crying out for this internal work from the inside out.

The major step is stop running away from this internal work and then balance can come naturally, but it is up to you to take on these challenges.

However, doing this work makes you a wiser person at the end, and then you can teach what you have learned along the way from your own journey of healing.

The real true nature that God had intended for us to solve our own problems—this is going in with a helping hand from God by asking for guidance of this work. He turns the key for you, and there you go inside of you.

Dana's photography titled *Inner Child Puzzle>>*

The inner knowledge of the soul that God has a plan for you but you have dug for the puzzle pictures and then uncover the real you and your soul purpose.

Mother and daughter's bond

8

Forgiving My Past

There have been life lessons uncovered about the choices that I made through growing up, and one of these lessons was with anger. This was a hard emotion when dealing with grief and loss. When trying to rediscover my own identity from my mother's suicide, I have discovered that anger takes on a life on its own.

The frustration and numbness took over every fiber of my being, and I noticed that when my frustration would build, so would the sandman over time. This sandman would hit the top of the lid and overflow onto other relationships, and then I would react to the outcome sitting in front of me as though I was the only sandman living with heaviness inside of me.

The depression would sit inside of me and then I would become numb. I realized that I was suppressing and repressing my emotions. In turn, the depression would be unsettled inside of me. I could never see the line of happiness unless I faked the internal happiness, which would lead me into outside forces that created havoc in my relationships and return inside of me.

The challenges seemed to be long and overwhelming at times, but at least I learned that I was looking for love in all the wrong places.

My focus has been about the lessons that I was taught from my father regarding restriction and discipline of thinking. This thinking always leads me to be in an action mode with deep issues of being abandoned by my mother, but I thought I had it all together as a teenager and young adult. But when you're at age in this precious stage of growth, you feel like Superman—or in my case, I was Superwoman, and I thought I knew it all and never wanted to listen, insisting on doing things my way.

I think I exhausted all those lines, but I realized that my dad had the best interest for me, and that was to guard me against making those bad mistakes as young teens and young adults do.

The one thing that circles back inward is the religion aspect of growing up, and I remember lessons about how to love through the lines of God, and it helped me grow from a troubled teenager into a beautiful adult.

Nobody told me that losing something so close to me like a mother could impeach the internal world for myself, and this seemed like an overwhelming thing I did hold on to when life seemed unbearable when the times of grief just simply took over me.

The aches in my body reminded me about the lessons about stress, and I must remain in relationship with God to help me heal all those pains. I had to reflect on those memories that I held very tight inside of me about my mother and even the small things that she said to me.

The sadness of reminiscing of my mother were the times that held me on a tightrope, and I looked down. I could see the ground, and I never wanted to fall in front of people again because I held high standards; but after a while, holding onto my numbness, I crumbled even at the smallest of things.

I saw the love someone had toward something they loved. It crushed me inside, and I began unknowingly keeping a record of things in my mind that just seemed to resonate in my mind of anger of my mother being taken from me, or at least that is how I programmed my internal thoughts when someone was achieving something and my mind was internal about my own self and loss and not working for me.

This made me realize that holding onto resentment kept me from climbing the road in front of me, so this was a big challenge with me until I realized that separating my anger at people and using projection of my internal world would help free me.

I was engaged in that my mind began to become small and forgetful and things began to fall to pieces in front of me, but I had to make certain choices about my own rational mind and come to terms that love was the one thing that I could barely hold onto but only with God's help. I have learned to understand what love means and what hate means.

It's easy for someone looking at you to say, "It's time you get over it," but when you are lost without an identity and love, you must create it in a world of feeling abandoned from the one woman that was my security blanket as a child and as a young teen.

My mother was my gift and in my eyes was everlasting, and no one can ever say, "Just let go and find love." If they did use this example, I would go internally numb and get angry at them because I just did not want to let go of what I really did love in the beginning stages of life.

The resistance phase of healing and my stubbornness creates stumbling blocks because I had issues with just wanting to let go of my love for her. I think the internal process began hurting my physical self because I would get all kinds of issues with my health, and all those systems would never make sense to me as they would come daily. After learning the efforts of the resistance mode of letting go and its effects, it made me begin to question my own authority of my body and thoughts.

My physical systems: backaches, legs tingling, digestive problems, dizziness and spells from time to time. I would always get hypersensitive when I would hear sirens of any sort and then my body would just react in shock and then I would create angry outbursts to someone else. It felt like my mourning process in those moments had overtaken me into another world all on my own, and this would make no sense to others; but as I grew into an adult, the same would appear but just different in reactions toward myself and others in the emotional roller coaster of relationships.

I still have health issues: appetite disturbance in which I feel like I am never getting enough to eat, and my body never seems to understand the discipline of eating healthy and how my mind handles my own stress because of the locked-in emotional phase of stress that overrides all things.

Then rush of grief runs through my emotional self, and those have become an intimate persona I wish I could let go of, but it does linger in me as I am faced with options and choices; but as time is the healer of things, I have become aware more of them than in my previous past.

This takes me to a list of the stress stages in which I am now learning to understand what phase my whole system is going through. It gives me reasons to forgive my past thinking and behavior as I cognitively understand this process in which my mother was going through when she committed suicide.

Three phases of stress: The *alarm stage* which begins instantly when my body becomes aware of a problem or situation that I feel I can no longer control, and so my body does this within seconds of my first initial thought or thoughts that race through my mind.

Second phase: my body prepares to run or fight, and so even though I am not aware of this phase, my heart rate goes faster and my breathing, perspiration, and blood circulation elevates and then my muscles tense.

Third phase: My body explodes with a high energy, and I use this system to express the desired outcome within moments of the rational and irrational moments of the first action of the alarm within me exhausted out of me.

When understanding that my body is reacting to my internal world of my body, then I can begin to understand the process which expresses discipline; but under other circumstances, I had no clue of what my body was doing in order to handle each social situation that was in my life. I had no clue that my body was sending me signals that it was taking charge when my emotional state was in so much havoc.

My level of stress would rise when my body reacted to the internal alarm system. "A change is taking place. Begin adjusting now."

Who would have known that my body was screaming to me and I had no real clue that stress could exchange so much information from my own thinking and coping from my mother's suicide and my own grief signals that run my body? My body talks to me, and I talk to it. "Who knew!" I had no clue that when my body would send out those signals. My ignorance or my lack of understanding within my own body kept me stuck. It takes shape even when I have no idea what is really going on inside of me.

Sometimes I think to myself, *Did not my mother really understand this process within her body? And if she did not understand this work, am I obligated to her and the help I need with myself of cleansing my internal world and guide her into realizations about the unconditional love currents that flow through our natural rhythms of a woman's body?*

Understanding depression with my body

Sometimes my body reacts subtle ways, and other times, I am faced with sharp and duel. This happens with me when the light causes adjustments in the eyes and my pupils become dilated. I become irritable with things around especially when my eyesight seems to go bad on me.

The intensity of stress outweighs the peaceful feelings, and then this is when my body is excreting extra weight from the flow of the environment around me.

There is another reaction in the lowest sense of the stress that gets me frustrated when my body temperature can't understand the flow of the natural rhythms of mother nature when my body gets cold. However, there are certain times that I experience internal struggles with loving myself. It comes when things begin to give into my adaption as a child.

The mind and body cross signals as the goal is within my grasp. There is a lonely side of me that

I could not comprehend because there was a lot of things that occur when growing without a mother. I had no idea that through the grieving stages, different things add up in smallest signs and symbols within my body. There is a chart which illustrates triggers of stress.

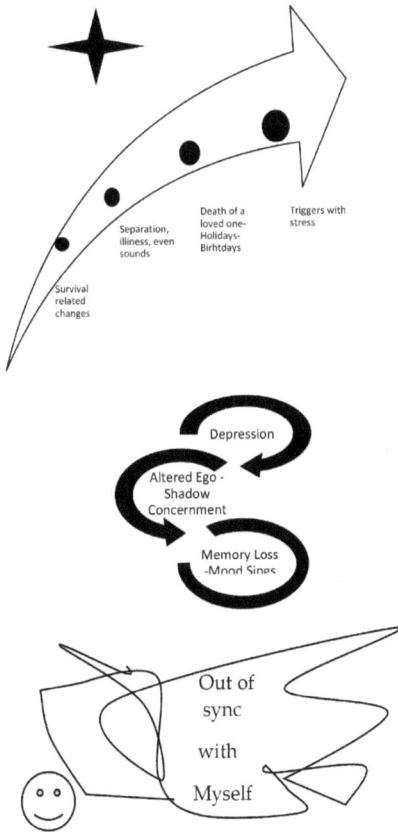

High-level stress scale

Dana's artwork of depression spinning within the soul and expression of loss and grief from a picture standpoint without words.

Healing comes when you let go—with unconditional love internally.

Mother and daughter's bond

9

Friendships

The balance of energy within is simply by adding positive friendships and the most recent accomplishments and using it to fuel your life with positivity. There is a question within myself about the quality of my own character, and so there comes a time of investigating the comfort levels within me.

Then my friendship with myself contains the angle of being stuck in a negative zone because of the low sense of self. I try to believe internally that there is a great woman inside, but I am just learning within my own character, and I must overcome this ruling aspect of myself through the means of positively rearranging my values system.

This is when my character grows and the friendship surrenders to a healthier life. This is rediscovering about my own values that I hold within myself.

Are my values and beliefs giving me a false sense of self and revealing the honest part of myself to other people and friendships? This is when I know that my personal close friendship can help and maintain in the recovery aspect of boundaries.

This is a good time to reevaluate the common greatness within myself, and how I accomplish this is by opening those values and reexamining those which insult my own view on things and when things don't feel exactly internally right for me. This creates a moment within an honest emotion, and in this gentle experience, it can give me a deeper desire within myself that I can rise above this with concrete evidence that I am self-worthy to achieve anything in life.

Friendship is a hardworking process, but if you overcome this obstacle and move forward and use the force within you to create a healthy sense of self, you have achieved greatness within this aspect of thinking, and the power remains inside of you. This is a great moment when friendship is coming to terms with the solitude of their own work and the rising from coldness to the extreme warmheartedness of love.

Celebrations and holidays with friends are understanding the field of nativity of who you are and the balance in which you are a unique person and have a simple greatness to achieve in this life. Yes, it is hard to overcome those battles in front of you; but once successful, it is everlasting, and this is what can happen with abundance inside a friendship.

The process of the healing is regaining confidence in which someone has stolen from you within those acts, but friendship helps this by adding a different side of viewing the pain. When you realize this and were very responsible to overcome with a strong focus of thoughts, you have used my method in which I have overcome the hardest battle, but my path has taken me into a higher walking method in which I will overcome.

This is separating more of what is you and what is not you, and then you create a vision board of what outcome you want to achieve. This is the greatness of your character within you. Taking steps in this process, you will rise and have the deepest knowledge one can achieve.

It's true—when you take the risk and jump into something, it means you must stand strong in the outcome of what truly lives within your heart. Does this mean if you want happiness on earth, you must first have it within you? Yes, to achieve this extreme happiness within the self, it is making sure you have a great sense of what is around you. Do the people in your inner circle have common issues with anger?

You must dig deep and find the nuggets in which these people are giving you a face value about yourself. What are those common themes, and what connection does it have with your path in achieving greatness?

Look for patterns which fit into the negative energy field and the common factors of what lives within you and use this as fueling point which can guide your heart to find a balance. This work is the hardest work but the most rewarding one ever that I have found in my own lifetime. You must overcome this mentality of thinking as this is in the moment by moment of keeping an iron control grip of outcomes within your own life.

This harmony is what creates the positive flow and the outcomes of creating life with value. This harmony can be dismantled by not examining your core self, and even when depression sits on one side of the fence, the other flip side is the friendship trying to create the harmony and balance back into it.

The friendship values are the game of life. If we have extreme negative values, we often tend to create negative outcomes. The friendship is a harder balance mechanism to keep healthy boundaries when one has consolidated negative reactions; therefore, there must be a neutral stance to maintain the key of flow.

If we have positive values, we often tend to create healthier values within ourselves. Create healthy values and a big dream and watch the outcome of life grow into a world of gratitude.

Mother and daughter's bond

10

Finding Love Again

Yes, the suffering of grief lingers through stages in the direction of love when a mother commits suicide. The action taken was out of force with self, and this can cause a ripple effect within the dynamic of the children and friends.

It is an act of selfish resentment toward the inner self, and when you have a daughter which loves the mother, she in turn takes on this role at a young age. It becomes a learned program response acting in selfishness and resentfulness and closing back in because of fear.

This is not a normal response in dying, so repercussions were not an act of altruistic love. It was based on in the moment of return and then in response to the world.

The internal world is screaming, "I am not good enough for you, God, and not even for myself." The shame goes through an internal shift, and the guilt plays a tug at the heartstrings from the altruistic God's love and manner of a mother's inner connection to Mother Earth. Altruistic love is spiritual, selfless, and unconditional, and the act of suicide confines this doorway of selfish behavior with a side note of resentment at self, and in return, love becomes hate.

These are the strings that are attached with me from my mother and the action taken in this life, and I feel it through my body and the spiritual connection of her and the remnants of the consciousness of my mother.

It's a hardening of love and the bitterness of sweet revenge at self, but intentions may not have been directed at the people she loved in this life, so the children are affected from an outwardly approach at them, but there is a grief side to this affection that children and family feel inwardly about their outwardly life. But if balanced correctly and healed through this, it can give a reason to understand love and what it really means to love from the life of love.

The storm can evolve within the family line, but healing and lessons about love is the key to the richness about the altruistic love of everlasting love. This is the God love everyone admires and adores. It's the genuine gift of just giving without expecting anything in return. There is no attachment in regard to the attitudes of the giving moments with this kind of love.

It is a different love than any other love in the world. It is at the purest form and the golden side of giving to the world around them.

Exploring the mixture of suicide love and altruistic love and the healing that comes with it

There are many reasons in which a person can hold onto the attached resentment when someone in the family or even friends create an unbalanced harmony from committing an act out of resentment. This action is about what they did not get or receive in the life that they wanted or desired, and the mind can design multiple stories which can cause internal conflicts with the self.

Therefore, the action was not on a healthy switch of thinking and rationalizing the consequences of this act toward the body. The reactions of others depend on the focus of love, kindness, honesty, and compassion in the response toward the individual.

The pureness of altruistic love guides the family or individual back into thinking about love, compassion, kindness, and even honesty. The grief tends to make a child more societal and more prone to be sensitive toward life when a mother, father, and or friend commits suicide. This can bring forth the love for self and internal love and compassion for others with a more compassionate side toward animals.

Now if the individual has a mixture of resentment and love, then the child has to understand what the differences are with respect to emotions toward others. The person who committed the act of suicide does depend on how the role will play inside of the child.

If it was the mother, then there will be more explosive emotional outburst toward love, and then the resentment will be expressed. This is how my mother reacted, and I am justified for the act she committed toward self, and so, therefore, I have the authority to give out what I know from the learned side of parenting of love.

The best direction in healing is to place awareness on the rational mind so it can explore what love is and what it is designed to do in the emotional experience.

The following healing has to go internal and separate the balance of those internal thoughts, and they must be worked to destroy the destructive avenue of emotions even during the mourning and grief stages. Otherwise, the child's inner beliefs are destined to recall the act on the emotions and make the actions come out, which is the resentment toward the people that love them.

Jealousy and resentment pull toward the inner conflict of not wanting to go deeper into the consciousness and dig into rational mindset and claim the gifts internally that God designed for the soul. If the individual uses methods of manipulations to gain more access of information, so the inner child does not really grieve in the right way, then depression rules inside of them.

The only way the inner child can resolve this problem is going deep within the soul and cleansing the pain and seeing that it is worth the pain as the growth happens. The beauty of the inner child begins to glow and reunite with the purity of love. This is the battle of knowing that love is the base in which all things function when the negative enters into any space. It has a job to do, and that job is only to divide.

If we can only see this as a whole.

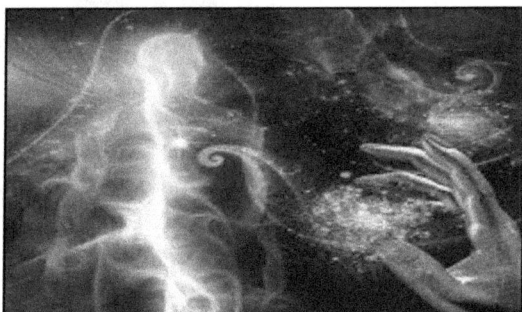

Reaching for the soul love.

Dana's artwork titled *Blessings Churning*

The flowing river is the sign and symbol of movement of finding the fueling moments in life, when life sensors are out of sync and we are claiming the unconditional love. Then blessings are coming into your life. Then life exists within you.

The jealousy is the surface layer from the internal self not engaged with achieving something and, thus, becomes the action of wanting to achieve, but the resentment gets in the way of their own achievements.

Thus, jealousy creates another explosion of grief because the child has no boundaries when it comes to accepting responsibilities and achieving goals to appeal the ownership of their own destiny. The inner child believes that they have this internal right from the parent that did commit suicide to not accept and achieve in their own journey because the action of the death is drawn toward the destruction aspect and not being appealed to the other side which is following their own journey inside of self-discovery.

The internal manipulation game with these children become lucid with the acceptance of the responsibilities in achieving for self. This is when the authority side of this character needs to pull back the strength and gain access to achieving something.

However, if the child is being put into situations of too much protection with love, this can also play a role in the abundance character of achieving and accepting life. It can be different than what lives inside of the internal love-focused mindset. This, in a sense, is using monopoly through manipulations for others to climb up the ladder for them so they can achieve and not deal with the internal self.

The self can and does achieve even in the smallest ways in life. The smalls steps make the huge ones look big in the moment, but it is actually admiring your own hard internal process of understanding the mechanisms of life and the internal space which is created for the loss.

The flip side of the coin of jealousy, envy, resentments on the scale of love is the deep understanding, kindness, acceptance of self, and compassion inside of the altruistic love. Loving the inside self is the focus of letting go of grief but in a healthy way.

Separating mysticisms in values or beliefs is another angle to learn how to trust inside of self, and love can grow into the altruistic love, and the depth of the soul's desires will be seen internally but understanding that we are all in it for "unity."

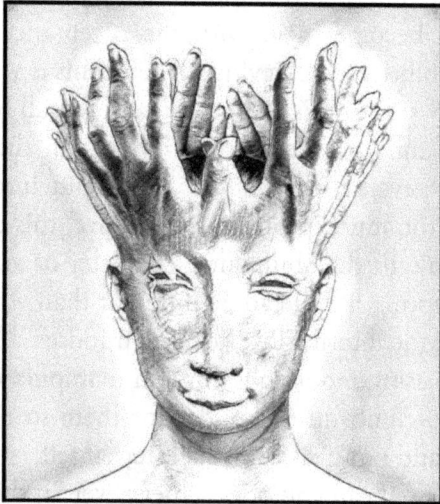

Dana's photography titled *Seeing Unity*>>

Life spreads with a breath of air and then we begin to ignore that we are all in it, as one unit within God, but it takes someone to receive this knowledge to be open to understand the basics of seeing unity within all things on earth.

Grief -Inside Hating Life

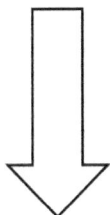

Spiral thinking

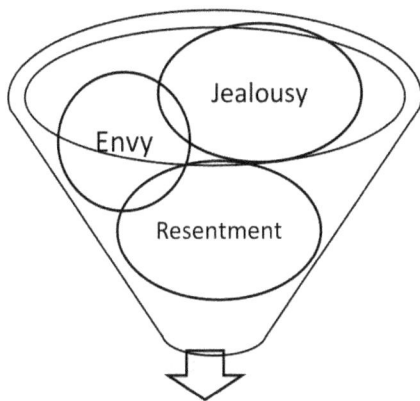

Jealousy

Envy

Resentment

UNHEALTHY BEHAVIOR

Grief- Inside Loving Life

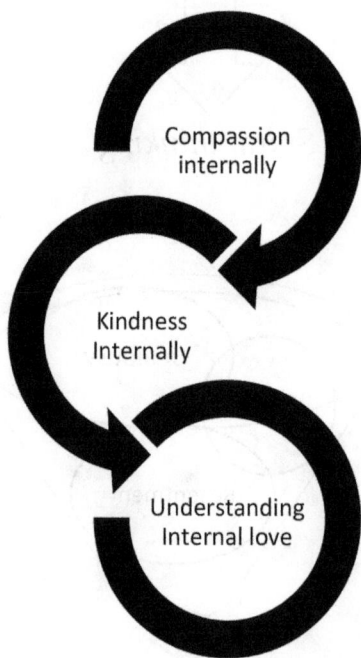

Compassion
internally

Kindness
Internally

Understanding
Internal love

HEALTHY BEHAVIOR

Mother and daughter's bond

11

Miracles in the Mess

Miracles happen every day. Change your perception of what a miracle is, and you'll see them all around you.

—Jon Bon Jovi

The deception of understanding life and death through a negative optical lens in my eyes gave me only negative viewpoints and then negative outcomes. This seemed to be the only avenue that I could comprehend after my mother decided her fate on September 28, 1976.

The balance game within me and the negative side of me began to be internally irrational about how to love inside of myself since I was thirteen and in a mess with all of who I was supposed to be.

Things just began slipping through my fingers as though there seemed like no control, and the emotions began to be overbearing especially after my mother's death anniversary after I turned thirty-eight. On this date, things just got more emotional than usual. This changed in my thinking and feeling as time went on.

Dana's photography titled *Mother's Extended Arms for Unconditional Love*

The emotional weight began to be heavier, and the level of comfort got tighter inside of me. I just felt like it was a suction cup grabbing me in and I couldn't do anything else but just survive in the mixture of things. This changed me as well. I got more afraid of being in the dark, and even at night, things just became more frightening than before.

It's like another life formed its own identity around me and I just responded. I began reacting, and the memories of my father reminded me about the stern focus which I was mindful of and which helped me through some major issues in my life.

Emotionally, I was connected to resentment and jealousy and just out of sync with who I was internally. All the things in my life began to just be a negative response, and I would try to accept things, but I just ended up rejecting them in then end.

I thought life just was against me, but what I found in going to church was that it was the inner connection of my mother contacting me and wanting to love me, but then something from the other side was attached to her, and it bothered me for years.

I rejected going to church and wanted to just sleep because I just felt tired all the time and just plain angry at life. I had to begin to find a miracle for hope that life was going to change for the better. I found a few churches that resonated with me, and the love began to feel like I could reconnect to a church and the people because I did not like sleeping all day and it was safe for me.

I began watching things on the television and some things would pop out of nowhere in what was going on internally with me, so I listened, and the miracles began to happen with me.

I began to trust what they were saying, and then life began to twist its ugly head into another frame of mind, which sprung open another door for me. Then I began to learn again about how to have faith in a destruction mindset. Life would pull me one way, and then frustrations would then edge me into something else. I just say, "Oh, just forget it and just stay home," and I did just that. I began to feel safety just in my own room and nowhere else. My bed was the safe space for me and that I just begged to be close by.

It came to me that death was the signal hand of what I was going through internally, and the mourning would pull more strings around me. The sensations of needing began to be prevalent, and the general side of things were lowered inside of me as though my internal wings were abandoning me.

I could not fly anymore—or least that is what I thought internally until I found someone to help me through this struggle, and then my eyes opened a little more.

Happiness entered into my space, and then I allowed the process to take place with the enduring love from afar, but there was a catch though. The need began to overtake me, and I created situations in which I thought I had no control, but I was fooling myself and was found out by a friend.

She told me that I was manipulating to get my way with anger, jealousy, and resentment. I did not want to acknowledge it at first because I was very much stuck inside of the law of denial. The question came to me: why would I need to change this dynamic because it works for me and I get people to do things that I do not want to do? It felt good to me to play the victim and then use the card of "I do not know anything, and I liked it."

It was like I was living my inner dream out and that was to live and make other people do the work and all I had to do was just get angry at them and use that as a weapon of choice.

The miracle began one day when the same friend walked over and said, "Straight up, I am going to tell you that I know what you are doing with manipulating me and other people with anger and resentment," and then I had to face the facts that I was not being honest with my actions and how I was hurting other people in the mix of love.

I thought it was a reaction for me to vent out frustrations, but I learned through my friend it cannot be this way. It was a hard lesson, but I found a boundary with it—the solid glove, as learning, to cleanse the inner walls of me.

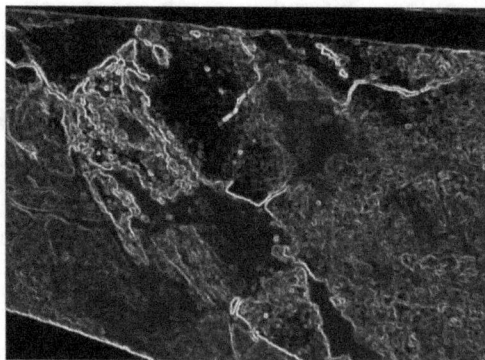

Dana's photography titled *Solid Boundaries>>*

When exerting solid foundations, after a loss, it tends to be a struggle because it's like we forgot who we were and then a wakeup happens. The urgency comes in hidden moments to enrich the moment with solid strength within the love of God.

Mother and daughter's bond

12

Holding the Shield

My mother's death took more twisted turns than I had thought it would go in my life, but I have found that after death, it caused inconceivable suffering throughout my journey of loving in life.

I guess I had many hills to climb and a lot of falling to get back up from the suffering from the loss of my mother. However, the focus driven has been about moving forward in my life. I have learned that survivors go through or enter a period of transition that normally lasts about four to six years, and each time it happens, I do shift my personalities inside of me through my infant, child, teenager, and to my adult self.

I have realized that are many stages of grief, and in this, I have learned that everything plays a role in everyone and even around me. It's like a sick disease that is hard to break open to eradicate it out of the body. There are things regarding the grieving stages of the bereavement process that I was unaware of and why I was going through these as though nothing seemed wrong in my life.

The early stages of bereavement is the angle of rationalizing about my whole self and the characters within me, or then I began to distort my emotions in grief and then the added emotions of rage, envy, resentment, jealousy, bitterness, denial, phobias, and so on. It would all take effect in this stage of my growth, and sometimes it still reaches some levels, but I think there is a little more control there in handling them.

This is my loss at the beginning.

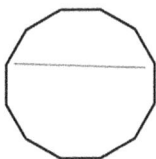

This is early bereavement stage which was jealousy, rage, denial, and bitterness.

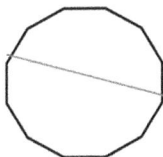

This was my release midpoint in the grief stage. My life was being restored at the greatest depths of healing because this was the lowest points in my life but the most rewarding internally from the growth. This was called bereavement midpoint.

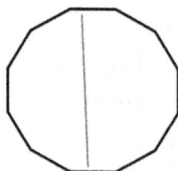

The next stage was trying to transition into completion, but those stages were very complex inside of me. My youthful and adult personality stabilized and found a sense of normalcy, but the stage which began to be extra hard and exhausting was the transcendence stage in which I couldn't relate to from the normalcy. I struggled with resistance, anger, and rage for the longest period.

The moments of wanting closure seemed to be far away from me. I think it was when I hit the transcended midpoint are the stages which began to circulate the midpoint. I had to come to terms of what governed my inner infant, child, teenager, and then my adult self, so this started to unravel in a group of ladies, and I found I could relate at a slower pace, but I felt like I fit in with them.

They helped me go through this phase of transcendence with adopting to their former selves and understanding the role which I needed to play. Then I came to understand their core values, beliefs and ideals, as well as concepts and ideas in which their model became more richer than my own and gravitated to grow and to continue to grow as I picked each thing that I needed internally for me.

However, I discovered the internal shield of resistance to change and that it gave a little bit of power, and so I hold onto the resistance as my shield for protection as I learn and grow within my own self and identity.

Mother and daughter's bond

13

Moving through the
Desperate In-Between

Here comes the test if I can endure the transcended midpoint and go further into my transcended beyond my loss, and this stage has been a
going phase of acceptance and make it out of denial:

Do I stay, or do I run? are the internal questions that my mind began racing through my
consciousness.

*Do I reject my own internal blanket of comfort or
stay stuck in my depression?*

*Do I keep in my own denial that my world as a
child and infant had complications from my mothers'
suicide?*

These began shuffling and became twisted in
the sense of what was right and what was wrong
internally with me. I began thinking something has
to be more than this pain level I kept on feeling, and

my former inner selves must be screaming for something every time I am getting frustrated easily.

The difficult task was that my bond with my mother was a very great bond, and so this also created the strongest bond inside of love.

I never realized, though, when my mother made her choice that she shattered the bond with heaviness of resentment and jealousy and it has been a roller-coaster ride to make sense of these stages.

After my mother passed on, it left a huge gap inside of our circle of bonded love. It created the depths of loss, and so I had no idea that there was a hole inside of me because she had left me.

This was at the beginning of the love bond together.

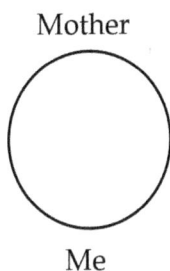

Mother

Me

Then when she left, this is how I felt:

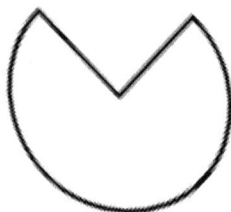

Me

Then when I realized there was a piece cut from me, I realized that my mother filled that other space inside of me because I had her locked into the bond and the love that was being formed back then with my infant, child, and teenager.

The cracks that kicked open the door of anger, bitterness, resentment, jealousy, envy, and the negative mood swings were being left from my own mother and the feeling from her death but also my own inner anguish that I have not dealt with in those stages of grief.

I think when my circle broke away from my mother and I lost my own self-identity in the mixture, the void began to grow into a huge bubble that I needed people to help discover that my circle was cut and that I needed to fulfill this void with goals and achievements which helps the process of learning to love without the circle of my mother.

I am still dealing with this broken circle, and sometimes as the bond healing of this circle happens, I am noticing that energy surging without any focus in my life, that it just lacks meaning; and every time I remove the light bulb from the internal side of me, then I notice that the lamp has no meaning either—meaning if the light bulb is dead and there is no energy added to it, how do I expect it to turn on when I added dead light bulb to the lamp with?

So some of things that I learned was to keep busy in things that I like to do and then also that I intelligently realized that our spirit (consciousness) crosses over and goes in a place in which it has to be doing something else than thinking about me. I had rethought about my time and devotion to her and her path of growth. This made me think that I am still holding onto her path and spiritually not allowing her to express her free will on the other side, when I was being selfish and resentful by holding onto old memories.

I have loved dogs for a long time in my life, and I love animals. I think when a mother cat picks up the kitten by its neck, it strangles it for a moment; but then when the mother lets go of the hold, the infant kitten can gain back free willpower; but as I have noticed, though, after the mother does this, there is stage of numbness, and then the kitten or even puppy shakes it off and then goes and plays.

This made me think about holding onto my mother like a puppy or a kitten and then I had to question myself.

Am I squeezing the life out of my mother by not letting my bond go between us?

Are there reasons why I am holding on so tightly, or can I just free her and be me?

Well, then I had asked my friends about letting go and getting a sense of what that was supposed to be as an emotional expression outward from the inward approach toward letting go of my mother. I began my stages of letting go, and it began to hurt, but I realized it had to be done for me and her.

Dana's photography titled *Reunited with Nature>>*

The soul splits off from the realness of love when a loved one dies, and this is the challenge that one must face in the mirror to reconnect and reunite with loving thy soul again as the self begins loving nature and the soul wins.

Love.

Mother and daughter's bond

14

Finding Peace

The delicate part is understanding the process of the inner world of my emotions and making sure that I am cognitively and intelligently breaking this open and letting go through each stage that needs to happen.

As children, we sense that life and death is like moving from California to Florida, and the distance between them are far between the two of these states. It doesn't make sense that it is only a couple of days of driving or a few hours of flying.

The mind of the child cannot see the path of letting go either. If the child feels like it is a major rock to remove, then the resistance becomes stronger, and the lightning bolts have difficulty to see through the elevation process.

This is the stage of letting go and then finding your own path, but as a child, it feels like the rock wins every time because it is so heavy and the strikes of punishment can no longer be dealt with as long as the parent is missing to do his/her part of letting go, so the child has to learn to cope on the level stages of an adult.

The child is the one who wants to rebel and can get aggressive when needing to get his/her way. The child has the gut reactions of running away, and if they are pushed into a corner, they fight with fierce rage at the one holding them back.

The child always wants growth and to learn something but only when the child is wanting to learn and be inside of the stage of learning and grasping new ideas. This is when the child is at play at learning and grasps the idea quicker than this long-drawn-out discussions about life and death.

The child running into walls, though, fails in life because they feel like they are failures, and then the self feels like a lower standard in life and that no one will accept them for who they are without jealousy.

This child has to know that when they feel strength and courage, to use it to go forward and not by using the force of aggression, rage, jealousy, or envy at other people. When the child can separate the two worlds, then life moves forward.

Egotism-conceit, self-importance

Low-self-esteem

Child's Negative Response

Division -Split- Loss

Lines through things

V.S.

Child's Positive Response

Unity

Love

Openness

Creativity

Curiosity

Mother and daughter's bond

15

Standing Strong with Courage

The layers of sensitivity go a long way when the child and infant needs self-growth. This is the psychological game of inner knowing wisdom and knowing how to respond instead of reacting toward things and/or people with egotism and negative child responses which is self-importance and self-ignorance. The adult self should know the inner wisdom of the two.

The child has issues, though, when the parent commits suicide because the egotism, which is the self-importance, and then uses the play in division and the split system of them being on earth. This creates the grief and loss between the child and parent which, in my case, was my mother, so I split off my female side when my mother left me in a half circle.

I began using the male-dominant side of myself as a clue into life since I had my father to give growth to me, so when my child, infant, and teenager climbs up and out, this is my internal process to get healing from the females around me.

Female healing is recognizing the nurture and nature side of things, which is regarding knowing how to take care of my inner teenager self, inner child self, and my inner infant self from a feminine point of view.

This means the female side has to be raised up, and the responsibilities is of the adult self by being the caretaker of all of the balance process in self and be organized internally with my female energy. This means the caretaker inside of me is a dominant character, but also authority side is spinning in a circle of a negative side and a positive side of thinking and reacting, knowing the protection side of the nurture side and the taking care of self and being skilled in the process of being a female with sensitivities and knowing how to resolve them through processing information, which is solving them nurturing and loving things, then hating things through the egotism side of things.

Reward

Loss

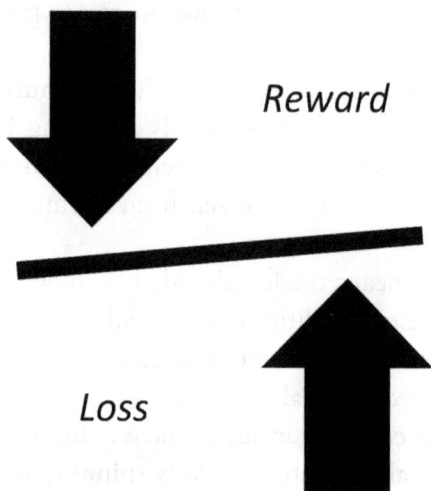

Almost every human experiences these two positions in life. Rather, it is on a scale of positive or negative, but a lot of it leads in the direction of death of a loved one.

The way to carry it forward is the more positive side, which is in the neutral thinking and feeling toward ourselves.

They both conceive of a mental attitude, and if you keep this in balance, then the flow of the soul can just glide effortlessly; but if there is a negative hangup, then the flow is erupted, and the balance of self leads to a mental fog and depression.

It can also express itself through the attitude.

Dana's artwork titled *Searching for the Garden Light>*

The sensations of investigating of the female light must come from the internal side of nature within me. I can find the flow of energy through Mother Nature and know that she has the altruistic love that I am searching for in this lifetime.

—Dana Gregory

Mother and daughter's bond

16

Holding My Own

The glue that holds—courage, love, strength, and abundance—is the level of honesty from the inner child's growth and loving myself. The balance and unity of God's laws through the universe is the focus of love and, in these laws, can change and sculpt me into the unity of God and as I am working through the sensitive side of the female and the dominant male aspect of myself.

I can discover there is so much more that I need to aware of than sticking with denial. The denial keeps me in the stronghold of rational and irrational mood swings, and it's a soul's journey to know when the mind is seeing the facts of mystical dreaming and the mysticism of thinking through my values and beliefs.

I have to be aware of the ins and outs of my reaction modes with my emotions but also being self-accepting of different comfort than my own to grow.

When I walk into the discomfort of sleep dreaming and walk into reality of the circumstance all around me, I have become visual about my future as I am holding my own and mindful of each step that I take. It is the walk toward the love within me first and then the walk inside of God to be fully accepted with all of me.

There were things in my life that never made sense until going inside and waking up the inner infant and inner child but mostly helping the inner teenager to mature into the adult self that I am today.

Growth comes when I open myself to understand the ways that govern my inner and outer worlds. I must take charge of all my responsibilities in my life in order to have organizational thinking and feeling so that way, my life can be more blessed in harmony and work toward the altruistic love—the love that exceeds all things which giving is through most selfless factors and not receiving anything in return and not even recognition for the act in itself. This is when I am getting closer to God and the love internal space that he shares with me.

The abandonment that occurred with my mother and my own characters within myself has to be dealt with in accordance of self-acceptance that I have been doing over the years has to change internally for the outer world to give me what I truly am looking for, which is the grace of God and the walk with him.

I know there is a deep challenge that I must undertake of making sure that I use the iron control grip over my emotions and expressions of them and then express purity of love toward others even when the outcome doesn't feel like it in the moment. I have maintained this to get internally closer to myself.

Then my work of the understanding nurturing side of me has to be balanced with my male-dominant side so I can find my center within God. I must seek inwardly and not outwardly to find resolutions which contribute to the inner healing through my infant, child, teenager, and the adult self. The adult self must take charge and get things done so I can have a dream of love.

Centering the base of myself is the challenge of letting go of my mother because the circle of me had a piece cut out of me, but if I rebuild my inner characters and find a hobby in which I love and then explore different avenues around me then saying, "I don't like this or that," and in this negative there will be a positive that comes from the inner work of knowing and sculpting the outer to make a difference of who I was when my mother passed but even now on whom the character that I have become inside and outside.

I do know that running away only just solves the moment and then I am faced with the stress of what I am running from. The stress comes from the balance in which I am not making for myself, and the actions to get there are the directions in which I must take in order to walk away from mistakes.

I have let go of resistance to change and the desire in which my soul is crying for the change, but

I use the iron control grip to keep the pain alive and which I must let go of. This is the other side of the coin which I must understand knowing who I am at the core of me. This knowing of the infant self and then healing my core is the work in front of me, but knowing God is helping and guiding me seems to take the pressure off me from knowing that I am not alone.

My split selves consist of working through them and resolving the karma and healing from this life and trusting that God is there, showing me the people who need to guide into the stages of love in order to be closer to him.

There have been many lessons in which I have had to learn about my character that doesn't fit into the glove of God and so I had to resolve them to certain degrees and then I come back to them and work on the knowledge which is managing those thoughts which get me into trouble of reacting within negative attitudes.

My attitude is everything which controls my comfort and the resistance of change. This is the angle which I find is the balance in which I will find my pursuit of happiness from God and my own infant self.

This is the longest work that I have to do, but I am finding that love is the center and I am around it; and when I am out of the center of myself, so is the love of God. But the most important factor is that I when have closed the door of God's connection within the love line, this is when life throws me to the curb, and I have come back full circle back to him for the forgiveness of just walking away from own self.

The one thing that has been on my mind here lately is that I did have a good life and that I don't ever want to change this.

I do know there is a spoiled side of me because of not having to go through as many challenges that others have been through, but I can persevere only if I change my love angle of being selfish. Then I may come into God's real love, which is the altruistic love of being selfless, and then my characters within the spoiled side of me will grow more and be more in tune with the center of God.

The embrace of loving myself and others is the call toward my present and future callings within my own path. The end results will help me end the cycle of ancestors and the karma that may reside within me and my mother's past love.

Two hearts—always bonded together
With forever love!
But
Two different female identities

Focused Intent Thought

Discipline

Iron Grip Control

Responsibility

Unconditional
Altruistic love

Leader

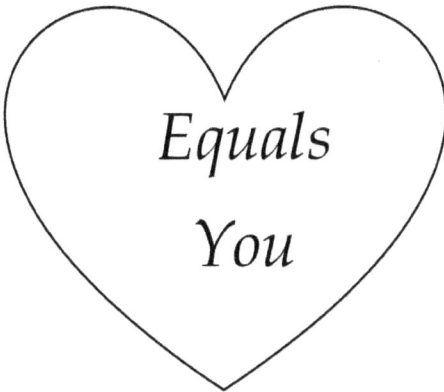

Equals

You

Fifty Laws of the Universe: You within God

Fifty universal laws

1. The Law of Harmony
2. The Law of Karma
3. The Law of Wisdom
4. The Law of Grace
5. The Law of Soul Evaluation
6. The Law of Bodhisattva
7. The Law of Vibrational
8. The Law of Free Will
9. The Law of One
10. The Law of Manifestations
11. The Law of Consciousness Detachment
12. The Law of Gratitude
13. The Law of Fellowship
14. The Law of Resistance
15. The Law of Attraction
16. The Law of Reflection
17. The Law of Unconditional Love
18. The Law of Magnetic Manifestations
19. The Law of Abundance

20. The Law of Divine Order
21. The Law of Attitude
22. The Law of Threes (333)
23. The Law of Association
24. *The Law of Commitment*
25. The Law of Dissidence
26. The Law of Experience
27. The Law of Fearful Confrontation
28. The Law of Group Consciousness
29. The Law of Personal Return
30. The Law of Activity
31. The Law of Denial
32. The Law of New Beginnings
33. The Law of Condensation
34. The Law of Psycho Influence
35. The Law of Totality
36. The law of Dominant Desire
37. The Law of Duality
38. The Law of Self-Destruction
39. The Law of Environmental Manifestation
40. The Law of Restriction
41. The Law of Self-Worth
42. The Law of Growth
43. The Law of Self-Truth
44. The law of Summarized Experience
45. The Law of Belief
46. The Law of Dharma Direction
47. The Law of Purify Action
48. The Law of Karmic Excess
49. The Law of Release
50. The Law of Ritual

Recommendations

Highly Intuitive Sensitives
Courses Work: Videos and Books

Heidi Sawyer

Heidi has given me great success with understanding my highly sensitive nature and knowing how to embrace things from this level than any other person. *Highly Intuitive Sensitives* are born with a higher vibrational frequency in which we came here to help the ones who struggle with their sensitive sides in life.

She gives it to you in a straight and honest way to handle things that disturb the frequencies with stress and many other focus points which affect us but also move us forward inside of meditation videos to go internal and release the blockages that bind us in the past.

I am grateful for these courses that are affordable, and the main thing is the effective aspects it sends back to you.

HeidiSawyer.com

Heidi Sawyer (YouTube)

"Energy Enhancement Course Work" and Meditation Videos and Books

Swami Satchidanand

Ancient Sacred Symbols are guided meditations indicating "how to get into alignment with a stream of energy from Kundalini chakra in the earth's center" to the central spiritual sun and "brighter than ten thousand suns" in the center of the universe.

Human Evolution and the Chakras Sexual Abuse and Rape

The Heart Chakra and Society Crown Chakra Connections Then There Is Anger

Jealous People Are Called "Monkeys"

What are the strategies of the energy vampire?

When the soul is out of alignment and chakras are being blocked, then the body creates illness and diseases and then death because the body is not supposed to go out of the alignment of the chakras.

This is also believed of how Jesus Christ began his teachings of the consciousness self and the immortal soul that is believed to be the craft and the connections into the holy God, which these courses take into the high self of God and to become more enlightened to be a son of God.

There is always darkness among us and takes us down and all this stress takes havoc on the body. The health decreases, and the alignment has been affected. The balance of harmony is out of sync and then the flow is gone and you lose energy.

There are dark forces and sources which attach hidden cords and suck the life force out of you. These courses teach you how to maintain them and then use techniques to banish all dark sources of evil that attaches and steals energy through the cords and the connections with you.

These courses help you deal with people with jealousy and envious people, but also it goes into many different phases of how to become hole and in the light of God.

sol@energyenhancement.org

www.energyenhancement.org

Energy enhancement live Courses in India, Spain, Mexico, Taj Mahal, Peru

Supportive Resources

Achor, Shawn. *The Happiness Advantage: The Seven Principles That Fuel Success and Performance at Work.*

Adams, David W. and Deveau, Eleanor J. *Beyond the Innocence of Childhood: Helping Children and Adolescents Cope with Death and Bereavement.* Amityville, NY: Baywood, 1995.

Allen, David. *Getting Things Done: The Art of Stress-Free Productivity.*

Alexander, Levy: *The Orphaned Adult: Understanding and Coping with Grief and Change after the Death of Our Parents.*

Arnold, Caroline: *What We Do When Someone Dies.* New York: Franklin Watts, 1987.

Arylo, Christine. *Choosing Me Before We: Every Woman's Guide to Life and Love.*

Aub, Kathleen A. *Children Are Survivors Too: A Guidebook for Young Homicide Survivors.* Grief Education Enterprises, 1991. 6971 N Federal Highway # 404, Boca Raton, FL, 33487.

Bailey, Joseph. *Slowing Down to the Speed of Life: How to Create a More Peaceful, Simpler Life from the Inside Out* (coauthored by Richard Carlson).

Bain, Burner. *The Book of Doing and Being: Rediscovering Creativity in Life, Love and Work.*

Bernstein, Joanne E. and Rudman, Masha Kabbelow. *Books to Help Children Cope with Separation and Loss: An Annotated Bibliography.* New York: Bowker, 1989.

Blackburn, Lynn Bennet. *The Class in Room 44.* Omaha: Centering Corp. 1991.

Bluebond-Langner, Myra. *The Private Worlds of Dying Children.* Princeton, NJ: Princeton Univ. Press, 1978.

Bolen, Jean Shinoda. *Goddess in Every Woman: Powerful Archetypes in Women's Lives.*

Buckingham, Robert W. *Care of the Dying Child: A Practical Guide for Those Who Help Others.* New York: Continuum, 1989.

Buscaglia, Leo. *The Fall of Freddie the Leaf.* Thorofare, NJ: Slack, 1982.

Campbell, Joseph. *The Hero with Thousands Faces* (The Collected Works of Joseph Campbell) and *The Power of Myth.*

Carlson, Richard: *Don't Sweat the Small Stuff... And It's All Small Stuff: Simple Ways to Keep the Little Things from Taking Over Your Life*—and the entire *Don't Sweat the Small Stuff Series: Easier Than You Think...Because Life Doesn't Have to Be So Hard* and *You Can Be Happy No Matter What: Five Principals for Keeping Life in Perspective.*

Cassini, Karthleen Kidder and Rogers, Jacqueline L. *Death and the Classroom: A Teacher's Guide to Assist Grieving Students.* Griefwork of Cincinnati, 1990. 1445 Colonial Drive, Suit B, Cincinnati, OH 45238.

Center for Attitudinal Healing. *There Is a Rainbow behind Every Dark Cloud.* Millbrae, CA: Celestial Arts, 1978.

Coles, Robert. *The Spiritual Life of Children.* Boston: Houghton Mifflin, 1990.

Corr, Charles A. and McNeil, Joan N., eds. *Adolescences and Death.* New York: Springer, 1996.

Davis, Betty. "Long-Term-Follow-Up of Bereaved Siblings." *In the Dying and the Bereaved Teenager,* Edited by John D. Morgan, pp. 78–89. Philadelphia: Charles Press, 1990.

DiPerna, Dustin. *Streams of Wisdom: An Advanced Guide to Integral Spiritual Development* (Integral Religion and Spiritual Book 1) (coauthored by Ken Wilber).

Dyegrov, Atle. *Grief in Children: A Handbook for Adults.* Bristol, PA: Taylor & Francis, 1991.

Fitzgerald, Helen. *The Grieving Child: A Parent's Guide.* New York: Simon & Schuster, 1992.

Furman, Erna. *A Child's Parent Dies: Studies in Childhood Bereavement.* New Haven: Yale Univ. Press, 1974.

Gaes, Jason. *My Book for Kids with Cancer.* Aberdeen, SD: Melius & Peterson, 1987.

Gaffney, Donna A. *The Seasons of Grief: Helping Children Grow Through Loss.* New York: Plume, 1988.

Gibran, Kahlil: *The Prophet.*

Gliko-Braden, Majel. *Grief Comes in Class: A Teacher's Guide.* Omaha: Centering Corp. 1992.

Goldman, Linda. *Life and Loss: A Guide to Help Grieving Children.* Muncie, IN: Accelerated Development, 1994.

Gootman, Marilyn E. *When a friend Dies: A Book for Teens about Grieving and Healing.* Minneapolis: Free Spirit, 1994.

Gordon, Audrey K. and Klass, Dennis. *They Need to Know: How to Teach Children about Death.* Englewood Cliffs, NJ: Prentice-Hall, 1979.

Gordon, Sol. *When Living Hurts.* New York.

Gottlieb, Sharpio. *A Parent's Guide to Childhood and Adolescent Depression.* New York: Bantam Doubleday, 1994.

Gravelle, Karen and Haskins, Charles. *Teenagers Face to Face with Bereavement.* Englewood Cliffs, NJ: Messner, 1989.

Gregory, Dana K. *My Healing Journey—Silhouette Whispers.* Xlibris Publications, 2017.

Gregory, Dana K. *My Healing Journey—Delicate Layers of Pearls.* Xlibris Publication, 2018.

Grollman, Earl A. *Explaining Death to Children.* Boston: Beacon Press, 1981.

Grollman Earl A. *Straight Talk about Death for Teenagers: How to Cope with Losing Someone You Love.* Boston: Beacon Press, 1981.

Grollman Earl A. *Talking about Death: A Dialogue between Parent and Child.* Boston: Beacon Press, 1981.

Grollman Earl A., ed. *Bereaved Children and Teens: A Support Guide for Parents and Professionals.* Boston: Beacon Press, 1995.

Gullo, Stephen V. and others, eds. *Death and Children: A Guide for Education, Parents, and Caregivers.* New York: Tappan Press, 1985.

Hartnett, Johnette. *Children and Grief: Big Issues for Little Hearts.* Good Morning, 1993. P.O. Box 9355, South Burlington, VT 05407- 93553.

Hay, Louis. *Heal Your Body.*

Hope, Edelman. *The Motherless Daughters: The Legacy of Loss.* 1995 Bantam Double play: Dell Publishing.

Huntley, Theresa. *Helping Children Grieve: When Someone They Love Dies.* Minneapolis: Augsburg Fortress, 1991.

Jewett, Claudia L. *Helping Children with Separation and Loss.* Boston: Harvard Common Press, 1982.

Kolehmainen, Janet and Handwrek, Sandra. *Teen Suicide: A Book for Friends, Family, and Classmates.* Minneapolis: Lerner, 1986.

Kolf, June Cerza. *Teenagers Talk about Grief.* Grand Rapids, MI: Baker Books, 1990.

Kiibler-Ross, Elisabeth. *On Children and Death.* New York: Macmillan, 1983.

Kiibler-Ross, Elisabeth. *On Death and Dying: What the Dying Have to Teach—Doctors, Nurses, Clergy and Their Own Families* and *On Grief and Grieving: Finding Meaning of Grief through the Five Stages of Loss.*

LaTour, Kathy. *For Those Who Live: Helping Children Cope with the Death of a Brother or Sister.* Omaha: Centering Corp. 1983.

Linn, Erin. *Children Are Not Paper Dolls: A Visit with Bereaved Siblings.* Incline Village, NY: Publisher's Mark, 1982.

Lombardo, Victor S. and Foran, Edith Lombardo. *Kids Grieve.* Ted Springfield, Ill, Thomas, 1986.

Lonetto, R. *Children's Conceptions of Death.* New York: Springer, 1980.

Lord, Janice Harris. *Death at School: A Guide for Teachers, School Nurses, Counselors and Administrators.* Dallas: MADD, 1990.

Metzger, Margarette. *Little Ears, Big Issues: Children and Loss Center.* 1991.

Morgan, John D., ed. *The Dying and the Bereaved Teenager.* Philadelphia: Charles Press, 1990.

Morgan, John D., ed. *Suicide: Helping Those at Risk.* King's College, 1987. 266 Epworth Avenue, London, Ontario, Canada N6A 2M3.

Murdock, Maureen. *The Heroine's Journey: Woman's Quest for Wholeness.*

Myss, Caroline. *Sacred Contracts: Awakening Your Divine Potential.*

Papadatu, Danai and Papadatu, Costas, eds. *Children and Death.* NY: Hemisphere, 1991.

Pausch, Randy: *The Last Lecture.*

Peck, Michael L., Farberow, Norman L. and Litman, Robert E. eds. *Youth Suicide.* New York: Putnam, 1986.

Raymond Moody Jr. MD and Arcangel, Dianne. *Life after Loss: Conquering Grief and Finding Hope.* Harper Collins Publishing, 2001.

Schaefer, Dan and Lyos, Christine. How Do We Tell the Children? A Step by Step Guide for Helping Children Two to Ten *Cope When Someone Dies.* NY: Newsmaker Press, 1993.

Schleifer, Jan. *Everything You Need to Know about Teen Suicide.* NY: Rosen Publications, 1988.

Schwallier, John E. and others, eds. *Children and Death: Perspective from Birth through Adolescence.* NY: Prager, 1987.

Schulz, Charles M. *Why, Charlie Brown, Why? A Story about What Happen When a Friend Is Very Ill.* NY: Topper Books, 1990.

Scrvani, Mark. *When Death Walks In.* Omaha: Centering Corp., 1991.

Slaby, Andrew and Garfinkel, Frank. *No One Saw My Pain: Why Teens Kill Themselves.* NY: Norton, 1984.

Smith, Judy and Ryerson, Diane. *School Suicide Prevention Guidelines.* Washington, DC: American Association of Suicidology, 1990.

Stillwell, Elaine. *A Forever Angel.* Omaha: Centering Corp. 2000.

Stillwell, Elaine. Sweet Memories: *For Children and Adults to Create Healing and Loving Memories for Holidays and Other Special Day.* Omaha: Centering Corp. 2000.

Traisman, Enid Samuel. *Fire in My Heart, Ice in My Veins.* Omaha: Centering Corp. 1998.

Vogel, Linda Jane. *Helping a Child Understand Death*. Philadelphia: Fortress Press, 1975.

Wass, Hannelore and Corr, Charles A. *Helping Children Cope with Death: Guidelines and Resources*. Washington, DC: Hemisphere, 1984.

Wolfelt, Alan D. *A Child's View of Grief: A Guide for Caring Adults*. Service Corporation International, 1990.

Christian/religious resources

Anthony, Nancy. *Morning Thoughts: Facing the New Day after Death of a Spouse Mystic*. CT: Twenty-Third Publications, 1991.

Allen, Marvin with Robinson, Jo. *Angry Men, Passive Men: Understanding the Roots of Men's Anger and How to Move Beyond It*. NY: Fawcett Columbine, 1991.

Curry, Cathleen L. *When Your Parent Dies: A Concise and Practical Source of Help and Advice for Adults Grieving the Death of a Parent*. Notre Dame, IN: Ave. Maria Press, 1993.

Swami Satchidanada. *Super Energy and Sacred Symbols: For Perfect Wisdom Enlightenment*, 1999–2008.

Swami Satchidanada, *Super Energy and Sacred Symbols: Gain Super Energy with Energy Enhancement Level One through Eight Initiations*, 2008

William, R. Miller and Jackson, Kathleen A. Practical Psychology for Pastors: Pristine-Hall, Inc. Englewood, Cliffs, NJ, 07632, 1985 .

Internet resources

1000Deaths.Com www.1000deaths.com. This is an outstanding website for those by suicide. It offers "Links for Lights" Memorial, support, resources, and meaningful guidance through material.

American Association of Retired Persons (AARP) www.aarp.com. Click on "Coping with Grief and Loss."

American Association of Suicidology (AAS) www.suicidology.org. Full range of services.

Center for Loss and Life Transition www.centerfor-loss.com.

Center for Renewal Personal Recovery www.renew.com. Educational site, and the focus is on crisis and management.

Centering Corporation www.centering.org. It houses a large selections of grief books.

Compassionate Friends Inc. www.compasionate-friends.org.

Crisis, Grief, and Healing www.webhealing.com.

Death, Dying, and Grief Support www.death-dying.com.

Dignity Memorial www.dignitymemorial.com.

Free Mind Generations (FMG) www.geocities.com.

Grief Healing www.griefhealing.com.

Grief Net www.griefnet.com.

Growth House www.growthhouse.org.

Hospice Care www.hospicecare.com.

My Healing Journey www.myhealingjourney.site. The overall of this site is the expression grief and healing from traumatic experiences and healing through art.

Neothink.com.

Neothinkvswikipedia.com. This is a focus-driven community about saving life and making a difference with recognition of people of the world.

PeoplePedia www.peoplepedia.world. This is a site to leave a legacy or a digital footprint of who you were in this life, and it builds the life story in which you want to create in this life.

StillGrieving.com. www.stillgrieving.com focuses on bereaved parents and grandparents who are no longer in the acute stages of grief.

Suicide Information and Education Centre (SIEC) www.sptp@siec.ca.

Suicide Prevention Advocacy Network (SPAN) www.spanusa.org.

Widow net. www.widownet.com. Information chat rooms and online support for widows.

Glossary

Abandonment – a circumstance in which one feels alone and/or leaving things or someone permanent or for long periods at a time. Intensity feelings of being abandoned or deserted and empty inside of the physical flesh body, and the emotions understand being left alone.

Alarm Phase – first stage of stress, the initial impact of crisis or change.

Alone – having no one present: on one's own

Anticipatory Grief – grief that occurs before the actual loss, as in the case of the elderly or terminally ill

Ascension – the act of rising to an important position or higher level

Attachment – the innate need to bond with another: a sense of connection between loved ones.

Balance – the state in which one can handle circumstances or outcomes with a natural state of mind and use iron control grip with everything of responsibilities, standing ground with respective accounts of boundaries and by using compassion and kindness in correct ways to help enrich self and others.

Bereavement – adaption period following the death of a loved one.

Closure – loose ends are gathered; the initial devastation or a certain aspect of the loss is resolved.

Complicated Grief – grief that has remained intense, prolonged or both: grief that interrupts or prevents normal daily life activities.

Copying – grief behavior, a learned response: the way someone contends with grief.

Depression State of Mind – derived from suppression and repression of emotional stability; it is also driven from having a low self-identifying of the real consciousness but is also seen with a low self-esteem and self-worth thinking and behavioral problems.

Denial-Consciousness – the choice to refuse reality then is unconsciousness well. Refusing to admit to or accept a truth or fact differs from denial in that the individual recognizes or is conscious of the existence of the truth or fact but consciously refuses to accept it as such.

Dissociate – where the part of the consciousness separates from the whole; thoughts or consciousness departs from the body.

Dysfunctional Grief – grief that prohibits growth by prolonged suffering, interrupts normal activities, or causes life to be normal as a way of living.

Exhaustion Phase – this is the last phase of stress; it totally breaks down, develops when stress is prolonged in the daily living in life.

Grief – a process that carries several various emotions—shock, anger, guilt, fears, and numbness which carry over into thinking and then behaviors in the sense of sorrow and loss connections but lingers in the longing and abandonment stages for the deepening phase of something lost within the consciousness. It also is carried into the every day of our lives which is loss of a loved one.

Growth – this is a process of letting go of perceived conceptions of values or beliefs within self and/ or others and increased knowledge

Innate-Inborn –biological, present from birth, not acquired or learned. (Attachment and grief are inborn; they are products of nature as opposed to being learned in life.)

Mourning – expression or externalizing grief; adapting to loss of a loved one or animal or objects in the daily routine in life.

Mystic – a person who seeks contemplation and self-surrender to obtain unity with or absorption into the deity or the absolute or who believes in the spiritual apprehensions of truths that are beyond the intellect

Mysticism – as an experience of nothingness, mysticism as any kind of an altered state of consciousness which is attributed in a religious way, mysticism as "enlightenment" or insight and mysticism as way of transformation, also known as a constellation of distinctive practices, discourses, texts traditions, and experience aimed at transformation

PTSD, Post Traumatic Stress Disorder – is a disorder that develops in some people who had experienced a shocking, scary, or dangerous event. It is a natural to feel afraid during and after a traumatic situation. Fear triggers many split-second changes that the body can't cope with which adds a stressor in the responses, and it reacts in a state of shock and anxiety from the events. It is a state of emotional turmoil until resolved internally from a death or shocking experience for the person.

Projection – it's judging others by one's own thoughts and feelings, putting one's own internal feelings, thoughts, beliefs, or values onto another person.

Religious – a member of a religious order or one who faithfully practices a doctrine

Resistance Phase – second phase of stress, resisting change results in breakdown.

Spirituality – believing in a divine being or a power higher than self; life practiced with compassion, reverence, conscientiousness, serenity, and joy; trusting that the world is evolving as it should in life.

Stressors – any circumstances that creates or dominates the thinking patterns that connects to emotional loss or abandonment emotional expressions or that creates evidence in the mind that is a stressful outcome of what is desired in life.

Thanatology – the study of death and dying

Trauma – a deeply distressing or disturbing experience and/or physical injury.

Transcendence – moving beyond one to another, elevated above the former; survivors grow beyond the person they were at the time of the loss.

Notes

Lori Weaver is an exceptional piece of artwork within her own character and how she has molded and sculpted herself into a beautiful woman despite the loss of her own mother.

She cleverly intrigues another soul to kindness and love from her perspective. This is a unique blend and a deeper understanding about loving the bond of your mother, and her sensitivities take you through a clarity of different values and that holding onto something so precious as a mother's love is everlasting and the bond is strong. The growth of learning to live with strength and courage has given her wings of flight. She has created a world of love with her husband and friends.

She is admired and loved through the process of her genuine character of forgiveness, and this is from the lessons learned through maturity.

Growth of a blooming flower takes decades to open, but when the flower shines, she expresses the divine light of God through her soul. When she is open and ready to embrace the challenges of letting go, it's always up to each soul; but if the conviction stands, then she will be an everlasting jewel and shines ever so bright as like God in the midnight sky.

About the Author

Dana Gregory is an award-winning and international published poet in numerous books from the International Society of Poets and Eber and Wein Publishing with a recent submission of "Who's Who in Poetry" for 2015 and also "Best Poets of 2016" and Acknowledging Trophy in 2017.

Dana is an author of her own collections of poetry called *My Healing Journey: Silhouette Whispers* and *My Healing Journey: Delicate Layers of Pearls*.

Dana is an exceptional artist in dealing with healing inside trauma through art. She investigates through the mental and emotional challenges that one can face in life about grief and even loss.

It takes courage to stand with conviction when dealt with a poker hand of dysfunctional liabilities in parents, but she has proved by using art as her muse to diffuse dysfunctional statuses of relationships within love.

For more information about Dana Gregory's poetry, art, and the healing journey, visit www.myhealingjourney.site

Additional Books

Xlibris.com and Amazon.com

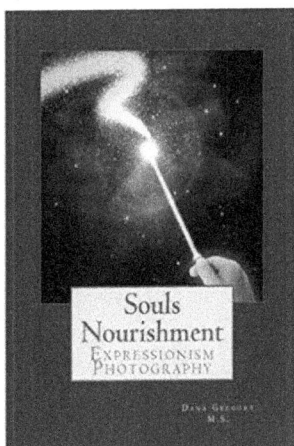